The Touch of the Earth

"Out of the threads of every day, drawn from the widely scattered substances of the earth, from our responses to earth, to man, and to God, we are continually weaving a fabric. We are ever translating and molding all that we receive into a creation that is our individual development and growth."

This is the beginning of Jean Hersey's book. A very personal journal of day-to-day living, **The Touch of the Earth** is about quality of life and the threads that make life rich and meaningful. Month by month, from the icy cold of January through the heat of summer to the warmth of a winter fire, Jean Hersey shares with us her observations about nature, life, and people. Reading the author's descriptions of birds, plants, and "little things" is an absolute delight. Some of her vignettes form a meditation of being which will cause us to rethink much that we often take for granted.

Jean Hersey now lives in a retirement community in Pennsylvania. She has published many books, among them are: **Carefree Gardening, The Shape of a Year, These Rich Years, A Widow's Pilgrimage**, and **Gardening and Being**.

THE TOUCH OF THE EARTH

THE TOUCH OF
THE EARTH

JEAN HERSEY

Phoenix Press

WALKER AND COMPANY

New York

Large Print Edition published by arrangement with
The Seabury Press

Grateful acknowledgment is made to
the following publishers for the use of
their materials:

Alfred A. Knopf, Inc. for the use of an excerpt from "On Marriage"
from *The Prophet* by Kahlil Gibran; Copyright © 1923 by Kahlil
Gibran, renewed 1951 by the Administrators C.T.A. of Kahlil Gibran
estate and Mary G. Gibran. Dodd, Mead & Company, Inc. for the use
of lines from "The Great Lover" by Rupert Brooke from *The Collected
Poems of Rupert Brooke*; copyright © 1915 by Dodd, Mead &
Company; copyright renewed 1943 by Edward Marsh.

Library of Congress Cataloging in Publication Data

Hersey, Jean, 1902–
    The touch of the earth.

    Originally published: New York : Seabury Press, 1981.
    1. Seasons—North Carolina—Tryon.   2. Country life—
North Carolina—Tryon.   3. Large type books.   I. Title.
QH105.N8H46   1984   917.56′915   84-15361
ISBN 0-8027-2481-7 (lg. print)

Printed in the United States of America

First Large Print Edition, 1984
Walker and Company
720 Fifth Avenue
New York, New York 10019

For Bob
Remembering this happy year together.

Contents

Jean Hersey wrote *The Touch of the Earth* several years ago. For personal reasons it was not published at the time it was written. Though time has passed and many circumstances pertaining to the book have changed the editors feel that it would be appropriate now to offer this book to her audience.

THE TOUCH OF THE EARTH

Keep a green bough in your heart
And the singing bird
will come.
> *—An Old Chinese Saying.*

To Begin With—

Out of the threads of every day, drawn from the widely scattered substances of the earth, from our responses to earth, to man, and to God, we are continually weaving a fabric. We are ever translating and molding all that we receive into a creation that is our individual development and growth. In our being we are continually contributing to the completion and fulfillment not only of our own souls but all those whose lives we touch, and whose reach touches us.

1

January Is Gold Stars in the Snow

YES, we do have snow in North Carolina. Our first of the season began about noon today, a fine sifting white powder. We watched it drift down against the wet and blackened tree trunks in our woodland. The white flakes fell gently, yet we sensed a kind of determination in the way they were outlining tree branches and small twigs. Our Japanese stone lantern grew a jaunty white cap; so did the bird feeders. Fence posts each acquired a little cushion of snow on top, while every picket wore its own small white crown. The benches made of long strips of wood and spaces between form a most beautiful geometric pattern of soft white lines and crosses.

Friends were coming for supper and, because of the possible driving difficulties later, they arrived at four. We ate Bob's delectable fish chowder, and fresh baked whole wheat muffins with orange rind grated in. All the while blowing flakes swirled in the glow of the outside light. If this kept on long we'd be snowed in! In contrast to the wildness outside there seemed an extra coziness within and also the beginnings of a pleasant feeling of isolation. The four of us settled comfortably by the fire, though only for a short time. Our guests didn't have far to go but still left very early and when they arrived home safely called to reassure us.

Three inches of snow here is like ten in Connecticut the way it affects the community. Schools close and everyone holes in. What will the character of this storm be? How many inches, and how long will the snow stay? We wondered that first night, but were not really caring. Usually it is only a day, or at most three or four. Then the sun emerges and we live in a dramatic world of whiteness and sparkle. In a few hours roads are clear. Snow here is invariably a lovely experience.

Before the storm the January jasmine was opening everywhere. Gold starry flowers in a tangle of arching green branches. The flower has six petals and a subtle, delicate perfume. They make lovely bouquets in the house. When blossoms fall there remains a green star of sepals, each with a shiny drop of nectar at the center.

Unlike forsythia, which unfurls all at once in a shower of gold, these jasmine blossoms come a few at a time, prolonging their period of bloom for weeks. The first unfold on warm, sunny days around Christmas, scattered along the stalks, one here and one there, a few together somewhere else. In several places around Tryon this flower grows in hedges, tumbling over stone walls and embankments—pure magic with hundreds of blooms out at once, each floret separated from the next and the starry shape clearly visible. All these blossoms will now be under a blanket of white!

Next morning snow is still falling but in a less businesslike manner. Tryon is paralyzed. No schools, no businesses function. Cushions of snow soften shapes, and the stumps in our woods are transformed into miniature Fujiyamas. We settled comfortably by the fire to write Christmas letters to friends and family. It's a little struggle to remember to put the new date on checks and letters. During the morning the door bell rang. Marcie, our neighbor up the hill, was sending fresh doughnuts by Sally, one of her five children. Making doughnuts is their old-time family custom for whenever there is a blizzard. And now, outside, neighbors' children, gay with red mittens and bright scarves, are pulling sleds and making snowmen. Everywhere angles are transformed to curves, rolling white curves, all with a glowing sheen. A curled brown oak leaf lights on the terrace, dancing and swinging over the snow surface while a misty sun emerges. The leaf is caught and turned upright like a flag, creating a many-starred shadow of brown fingers. Soon neighbors begin to telephone. "Have you enough food? Are your utilities OK?" Bob shoveled from door to street and we walked out to look around at this new and lovely world. A few sharp green spears of yucca were emerging from a great mound of white. A soft weight of snow hung on the Burford holly. On the millstone was a jaunty white birthday cake. How quiet and beautiful it all was, and how pleasant that we had no place we had to go.

John and Homer invited us across the street for an odds and ends lunch which turned out to be a delectable feast—roast lamb, corn pudding, beets, peas, mashed potatoes and ice cream. We all sat around their fire and talked until mid-afternoon. They were enjoying their holiday. How could anyone show real estate in the snow? Their cars were well covered and they had no intention of stirring.

Observing a car in the ditch across the hollow easily convinced us we should remain at home. After dark, we turned on the outside light and watched the snow blow. The constantly changing shapes and curves were fantastic. Before morning we heard the plow. Next day the sky was blue, the sun streamed down, turning the road, as the snow slightly melted, to glare ice for it was still below freezing. In two days it will quite likely be gone, the temperature probably fifty, and we'll be eating sandwiches on the terrace. This is Tryon weather. Temperamental. In Connecticut we would have struggled to keep mobile. But here everyone relaxed and enjoyed. I cleaned cupboards, cooked chocolate bread pudding and asked neighbors living within walking distance over for dinner, and we told tall tales around the fire. Thus the New Year came blowing in on a snowstorm.

Betty, a Haiku enthusiast, telephoned to give me this special message, a Japanese poem written by Shiki.

> I give thee Greetings
> Of the bright New Year
> As though I held
> A plum branch

The new year ahead is as fresh and unfulfilled as a bare plum branch. How can we know what will unfold these next twelve months, what flowers, what fruit? What directions and events will form in the new and untried weeks, days, and hours to come?

"That which is deeply personal is universal," writes Anaïs Nin. Will what I feel and share here, since it is so personal, waken, touch, and find a response in your deeper feelings and thoughts? Will some of the things we yearn for be what you also seek? Do you find joy in some of the same simple experiences that delight us, make us happy and richly content? Does some of what occurs in our intimate world find a counterpart in yours? I hope so, for this brings all people everywhere closer and helps us to realize that, in basic values, needs, joys, apprehensions, we all have much in common.

I'm forever discovering new things about cooking and kitchens. And incidentally winter is a good time for cooking. An amusing incident today brought to mind and use a recent kitchen discovery. Bob was away and I was cooking my noon dinner and had just put lima beans on to boil when the phone rang. A friend was calling to discuss with me the difference between a willow oak and a water oak when the door bell rang. I left her on the wire and opened the door to a polite woman who said she was from Kansas and just loved this community—didn't I think it was a beautiful place to live?—and how could she get to the top of Hogback Mountain?

I told her all the lefts and rights and she departed while I returned to the tree conversation. Before we could resolve it satisfactorily the door bell called me again. I left my friend on the wire.

"Did you say first left or right?" my Kansas caller inquired.

I went over it all again trying not to be impatient. "Oh, heavens," I thought, as the woman left, "my friend and the oaks!"

She was still on the line. We were just resolving trees when I smelled them—the beans.

"Oh, my, I have to stop," I exclaimed, rushing to the stove just as the smoke was rising. I snatched them off and dunked them in the sink, turning on the water. Ruined— all those lovely lima beans—and my lunch! And the pot! Black—and the bottom layer of beans burned into it.

"Never mind," I cheered myself, "no use weeping over burned beans." My mind was still a swirl of oaks. And here my recent discovery came to the fore. I dumped the beans, scooped the loose burned ones out, filled the pan with cold water and put in one-half cup of Clorox and left them. By night the pot was pure, glinting stainless steel again, with all the crumbles of burn having entirely disappeared. The miracle of all time!

What a wonderful Sunday. It began in the

adult class that meets the hour before church. About thirty people gather and share ideas, experiences, feelings, on a chosen subject. Our minister leads it. The current subject is love and grace.

It's fascinating how people view the same thing so very differently—be it a landscape, an event, a book, or an intangible like love. The discussion started with love and somehow grace merged into it. And then the question came up of what grace meant. It means such different things to different people. To one man grace was something that you called upon to see you through difficulties and crisis moments. To me it is something that happens that I can never call upon nor expect. It comes, maybe, when I step outside in the early morning alone to greet the rising sun. It is there in the form of a lovely feeling of oneness with all around me. Perhaps I sense it when my hands are deep in the earth and I am planting and weeding. I may feel it when I touch a friend in warmth and affection—when something happens between us and we realize what a good relationship is there. It may be simply when I'm walking through the house and see the sun shining in on the old-gold carpet, bringing a rich glow to the room. I might be looking at the woodpile outside that Bob has cut and stacked. I have a special feeling about woodpiles, and wood, and the potential fires waiting there in every log.

All these moments quicken something in me and for a few instants I am lifted above the ordinary. Is this grace? How unimportant words are, actually. I see this more as an awareness of the presence of God according to what God means to me.

And then there's love, about which volumes have been written, poems, songs, sonnets, an infinite number. The Indian poet Kahlil Gibran says "love is work made visible." Perhaps one can never limit love by trying to put it into words, it being essentially a feeling experience and not a thinking one. To me love is enthusiasm, warmth, caring, giving where you care, and also, and equally important, giving where you don't care at all.

Love is also listening *beyond* words to the person speaking. I find I tend to be caught in the precision and definiteness of someone's words, rather than taking them as an expression of where he is and how he's feeling at the moment only, knowing he may feel differently tomorrow.

I believe it is especially needful, if an individual says something that hurts, to be able, or at least to try, because it isn't easy, to see beyond his words to what is going on within him. If a person says something thoughtless and unkind the chances are this person himself has been badly hurt. "In areas of the world where the bee has no enemies it has no sting," writes Gerald Heard.

Someone who's a bit barby and tends to speak roughly to others can have been very much hurt along the way. If I can be aware of this at the moment this individual is saying something that makes me unhappy it keeps me from being too completely thrown.

Of course at the moment I am hearing critical words it's almost impossible not to feel a real sting and curl up inside into a tight knot. Hopefully, I will someday be able to maintain a part of me ever inviolate, separate, and in peace, especially in the midst of a storm.

Later, much later, I can cool off and consider what's happened from my friend's frame of reference and what's going on within him or her. I'm really making an effort to discount any unpleasant remarks that come my way, trying in the moment to hear beyond and feel and sense my companion's depth beneath the surface scratchiness. I know that hurting words can be an announcement of where a person is at the moment, and they don't necessarily relate to me at all. I'm only what triggered the words.

I recently came across this, the source anonymous. It seems to me a good thought for the beginning of another year.

May you have
    enough happiness to keep you sweet;
    enough trials to keep you strong;
    enough sorrow to keep you human;
    enough hope to keep you happy;
    enough failure to keep you humble;
    enough success to keep you eager;
    enough friends to give you comfort:
    enough faith and courage in yourself,
        your business, and your country to
        banish depression;
    enough wealth to meet your needs;

enough determination to make each day a better day than yesterday.

January is the time you especially appreciate friends. In the inclement weather we draw indoors and do more visiting. We have company for dinner, go out for dinner, walk with friends, talk with them, visit with them at our house or at theirs and on bad days sew or embroider by their fires or ours.

What does friendship mean? What does it bring and what are some of the hazards and delights in knowing someone really well and being close to him or her?

All the way through life we keep gathering new friends. Alas, we also lose a few. Sometimes by geography, sometimes by diverging interests. We've kept up with certain ones over the years by letter when that particular person has a flair for letter writing. But many whom we love simply are not at home with pen and paper, and then it becomes more difficult to keep up the relationship.

Betty Frost and I maintained our friendship for thirty-five years, but not by frequent correspondence. Maybe twice a year we would exchange letters, nice and newsy hers were, and I loved getting them. It kept us close. And the friendship flourished and grew during occasional visits back and forth from Tryon to Connecticut. But I can recall other early friends that I dearly loved who were not letter writing types, and I have, unfortunately, lost track of them.

What is fundamental to a good friendship anyway? Love is tossed about rather freely these days, but still is an important word, a vital quality, and the cornerstone of any friendship. Loyalty, giving of oneself, and forgiveness are surely fundamental elements in the love of one person for another. Consequently, these are essential nourishment to a growing friendship.

Recently I was rereading Thoreau's essays. The one on friendship is magnificent, and gave me a fine checklist. Was I following his precepts in my friendships?

Do we "cherish each other's hopes"; are we "kind to each other's dreams"?

Thoreau also wonders of his friend, does he "love and praise my aspiration rather than my performance?"

How fine to have as close companions

those who "look whither I am looking and farther."

These last two seem to me especially significant. The first inclination of many of us, I fear, is to see where a person is, and what he is doing, and then look no farther.

From this nineteenth-century philosopher we can glean an enlightened concept of what friendship can be. And new directions to work toward in relating.

Needing each other is also fundamental to deepening a friendship. The needing, to be sound, must be mutual. The best of relationships are those of equality in this regard. A trust that enables a sharing in depth also builds a lasting companionship. So does the ability to withold all judgment. I know I have to learn to restrain my quick assumptions. When a friend says or does something it is all too easy for me to jump to a conclusion: she's being thus and so. And maybe she isn't at all, and I shouldn't so hastily form an opinion.

Like all relationships, friendship is never static. It never reaches a peak and stays there. A live and growing companionship is always building, deepening, developing, and, alas, sometimes diminishing.

With some friends we play, with others we think and communicate on a deep level. With certain ones we *do* and engage in mutual outer activities. Some we walk with, some we talk with, some we laugh with. And how valuable are these latter! A number we enjoy in foursome or larger groups. A few women friends I like to be with part of the time alone.

We all have friends on many levels. I am thinking of the wonderful people in the Garden Club I belong to. Some I have come to know well, but many others I see only at club meetings, and yet I am fond of each one.

There are people who make us feel less than we are. The tendency is for us to out-picture their impression of us. Being with them is a real challenge to see if, in spite of this, we can stand tall and be our true selves. Then there are those who make us feel more than we are in ways that we can't quite define. It is this *intangible* more that is an exciting part of any relationship —to seek and find the "more" in ourselves and in another.

Surely we all have the capacity of being more than we are—and certain rather special people bring this out. When you feel that way, for a time then you become so. And the good feeling lasts. Again I find Thoreau puts it aptly. He aspires to have his friend

But be the favoring gale
That bears me on,
And still doth fill my sail
When thou art gone.

Each new person we meet is like a fresh and unexplored country. Even as we come to know each other well, we never really find out all about another person, nor do we ever want to. If we think we know *everything* about someone else it is because we are cramping that person into our own limited concept of him. The suspicion of unrevealed secrets in another's nature is part of his appeal. It is these unexpected glens and forests, peaks and valleys, that surprise us constantly and make any relationship a fresh and exciting voyage of discovery.

Some people are like fires from quick-burning kindling. The sudden rush of flames and sparks soon dies and the blowing ashes scatter. Others are like fires with a great bed of coals. Only a few flames may attract attention, but come close and you feel a radiating warmth and know that here is a vast bed of live and glowing coals, so substantial and enduring it can rekindle any whose fires of life are at a low ebb.

Often in a marriage one partner will be one kind of fire, and the mate the other. Each can draw from his partner. Coals need the kindle of fresh wood occasionally. The flame fires need the dependable quality of a bed of coals, and the world needs both.

Haven't you a friend who is like a cactus, whose flowers are rare and beautiful? But if you come close you encounter sharp spines! There are also those who live behind forbidding walls. Sometimes the walls are of words. These are the incessant talkers in our lives. Such people are usually a little lonely, and yet it is difficult to relate to them. The avalanche of words holds you off.

"You talk when you cease to be at peace with your thoughts," writes Kahlil Gibran.

Some friends stand off, hesitating to become involved. There is a risk in becoming fully involved no matter how fond you are of the person. But then, as Ibsen says, "There is a certain risk in being alive and the more alive you are the greater the risk."

Why not take a chance and be as alive as possible? What if it does make us vulnerable, and we are occasionally hurt? A scratch here or there soon heals. There is a kind of learning and growing that comes as we are able to bridge back, high over a misunderstanding, to the solid ground of how things were before.

People's traits, I am gradually discovering, belong together. If you find a quality in a friend that bothers you, turn it in the sunlight of your perceptions as you would a crystal in your hand and you will find another side, and different manifestations of the same characteristic.

The slow and steady person may resist new and unexpected ideas, but he is the Rock of Gibraltar, and how often we all need a little firm Gibraltar influence!

The quick and volatile man or woman may also at times be nervous, restless, and tactless. But turn the crystal and you find someone receptive to new ideas, and filled with fresh inspiration. Anyone who criticizes readily may have a low opinion of himself. He builds himself up by diminishing another. He may also have fine judgment and be keenly analytical of situations and events in a wonderfully stimulating way. Those who laugh a lot and love the world and everyone in it may occasionally be a little overtolerant, careless of time commitments, and overindulgent of themselves and others. We have to watch and not impose on these friends—or let them impose on us.

In a difficult encounter there are two recourses. First, try to figure out why your friend feels and acts as he does. This takes the heat out of a quick negative judgment. What is the background of these unpleasant (to me) ways? And next, look for what else is in the bundle. What other elements are there? We need to accept the whole package. But we can focus on the congenial and positive qualities. Both these procedures help us to be more accepting generally.

The affect people have on us is amazing, disheartening, exciting, startling, frustrating, and thrilling. The affect that we have on others can be all of these things too. How careful and concerned we need to be in what we say and do, with extra consideration for another's feelings.

To have acquaintances and contacts by the score can be gay and gratifying to the ego. To be greeted warmly on all sides when you walk into a neighborhood concert naturally makes you feel good, and gives you a lift. These moments are a beam of sunlight here, a flower there, a quick instant of passing joy. To be appreciated as such.

For the long haul those with whom we have a real relationship are the ones that nourish and sustain us.

When you are low-spirited, sick or lonely, those whom you only see at large parties or public gatherings are but the frosting on the cake, and make poor daily fare.

Certain people in our lives meet special needs in each of us. And we meet the needs of others, sometimes in ways we know not at the time. I remember going to see a neighbor, whose wife was in the hospital, and wondering how I could cheer him. For many years we had shared gardening lore. After my first inquiries we spoke not of his wife, but of the garden, his and ours. He did most of the talking, and I left wondering if I'd been any help at all. Some weeks later, when his wife was home and well again, he said, "You'll never know how much it meant to me that day you stopped by and listened to me. I was so worried about Susan, and I got my mind completely off her and felt better about the whole situation." I had feared I'd failed him as friend and neighbor. Had my recent resolution to be a better listener been more effective than I knew? How often we all have a need to be listened to, and how often we all need to listen.

Adventure in capitals is built into Pam's nature, and it radiates. Anything from a swim to a walk in the woods to making a soufflé together turns into an experience. We share hilarious times, and occasional other times in a serious vein. After I've been with her a few hours I feel relaxed for days, and on the crest.

Wonderful friendships develop when you do something creative together, play the recorder, learn a language, go painting, settle to cooking. A shared gardening enthusiasm also draws you close to another.

On moving to a new area, as we did three years ago, we met many new people. With someone just met we are both at the start of a totally new path. I have upon occasion wished my new friend and I could speak of things on a deeper and more significant level. But I have learned not to rush a beginning friendship lest I stumble and lose the way. I have to curb my enthusiasm, be patient and try not to be ten miles down the friendship road when, in reality, I am only one.

It was a golden day from start to finish! Just one of those that come along once in a while and lift us up to a new height where we may linger for a few hours or longer.

"Let's go to Green River Cove for the day and picnic, could you?" It was Betty on the phone.

"Of course, and what a great idea," I responded, watching out the window where a tufted titmouse was sitting on our feeder with a sunflower seed in his beak. It was a fabulous morning, in the fifties and promised to be warmer. Our erstwhile snow was long forgotten. It appealed to me not only to spend the day with Betty, which I love to do, but in January to be off for an outdoor picnic and a wandering, exploring day. Especially so since Bob had gone north on business for the week and I was alone.

Betty and I set forth with sandwiches, jugs of water, thermos of hot soup, blankets. The air was fresh and invigorating.

The Green River is really green. Rushing madly down its bed and curling over stray rocks, it sends little slim triangular streamers of white foam reaching out behind each one. The water surface was a pattern of green with small white flags darting all through it.

Great rhododendrons border the shores, and reach back into the woods to mount the cliffs. In a succession of coves we kept coming upon small log cabins with large, appealing stone chimneys.

"We've got to come back again and paint here," I said, and Betty agreed.

Now the mountains drew nearer, each tumbled ridge rising close to the next, and all tossed together, soft and almost furry as the sunlight sent shadows stealing over the tree tops. The summits of the ridges were fringed with a line of tall trees and a blurr of sky was visible between bare branches.

With the leaves off we could see way into the woods as we drove past; could see deep into the dimness to huge boulders blanketed with ferns. Christmas ferns in neat green rosettes were strewn along the roadside, and over the woodland floor. Delicate black-stemmed ebony spleenwort clung to banks where great cushions of green moss hung interlaced with gray reindeer moss. Now here were many different kinds of moss, some long and deep piled, some short and sleek and golden green. Gray fairy cups we saw in abundance too. And leather grape ferns, putty leaf orchid leaves, and the foliage of the crane orchid. And round plump leaves of wild ginger.

How far away from civilization we felt. We had left the cabins behind now, and the road, gravel and dirt, wound up and up toward Saluda through a series of switchbacks. The Green River lay curving below us in the valley. Beside a stream we stopped and got out to look more closely at some walking fern. We were near the car when we heard something in the underbrush—a dog, perhaps? Turning, we caught and held our breath—a deer was heading directly for us. Seeing us, he stopped but a few feet away, and quickly changed direction. With a graceful leap he swung off down through the trees out of sight, flinging up his tail. The underneath part of his tail was snowy white and seemed a yard long. In spite of his quick departure the memory of him lingered. He had been near enough for us to see his soft smooth coat, tawny as the meadow grass in winter, and his beautiful sensitive face, his eyelashes, and his quiet eyes.

There is something breathtaking and awesome about an encounter with a creature of the wild. You realize that we are, in a way, only trespassers. The woods belong to the wildlife, these mountains and coves are nature's province. Intruders that we are, we should tread lightly and with respect and not disturb nor destroy.

But such a meeting does more than this. Where had the deer come from, where was he going? Where was his mate, his companions? Would we be lucky and see another deer today? The answers to these and many more such questions come blowing down the valley in the soft rustling breeze, and spilling over the mountainsides in little waterfalls. But who can translate?

We walked a ways up the road. Now and again a car full of hunters passed, men with red coats or caps. We pray our friend escapes. It is queer how many terribly nice people are hunters. Of course, *we are all* rather inconsistent. We eat beef, and chickens, and fish, and yet why does something in me hurt and shrivel at the thought of hunting and killing a deer— those beautiful creatures? How can people do it?

Presently we heard shots.

Oh, no, it couldn't be *our* deer. He must be far, far off by now.

Soon we found ourselves sitting in a sheltered spot on the blankets we had brought. The sunlight was beaming down upon us. We were starved after our walk and woods wanderings. How good was the hot soup and turkey sandwiches, and the crunchy cookies to end with.

We began discussing the different birds we were hearing, and wondering what sort of bird we'd like to be were we one—with Betty it's always easy to wander into such fantasies.

"A wren," I said. "A Carolina wren because I'd like to be able to sing the kind of song they sing."

"That means you are home loving," Betty said. "But I guess I already knew that—"

"What's yours, what kind would you like to be?"

"A water ousel, because they sing all year and have such fun in the water!"

We both decided we'd enjoy being squirrels because of what exhilaration they must feel up in the tree tops swinging from the tip of one branch over to the next. Always sure and never slipping, yet way up there high, almost flying—

After lunch we stretched out in the sun on our blankets, relaxing, and watching the trees overhead and the clouds, listening to the stream, the birds.

"Look," I said, "if you watch the tree tops and clouds in a certain way you can imagine the clouds are standing still and the trees and the earth here where we are lying is moving and us with it. You can feel yourself a part of the turn of the earth—"

For a few moments we did just this, an eerie feeling, and then all of a sudden I want to be back to the way things are. I want those great trees and towering rock ledges to be still and steady and the clouds to be coasting across the blueness.

Time drifted on till we finally gathered ourselves together and set out for home. On the way down the view of the cove below was beautiful. All the way back we caught changing vistas of mountains, with the shifting sun touching highlights on different trees, slopes, and valleys. An especially magnificent experience with the car top down!

When we arrived back, and told Norme about the deer with a yard-long tail, he said in his good, solid, down-to-earth way, "There is no such thing, deer tails are never longer than fifteen inches!"

"That just goes to prove," I replied, "that where we were was a truly enchanted spot! There was magic all around us this day."

2

February Is For Ruminating

DOWN in the cellar yesterday I discovered treacle!

We have a friend in England who is slightly mad in a wonderful sort of way. We met her and her husband a few years ago on an alp. We were all staying at a little mountain inn in Switzerland and used to hike together. Ever since and periodically she sends us presents, creating a sort of perpetual Christmas. It may be a book she thinks we'll like, exotic earrings for me (she's rather an exotic person herself!), a special kind of shoe polish for Bob, or a hand-embroidered tablecloth and napkins for us both. Something deliciously unexpected can arrive by mail at just about any time.

The summer we visited them in England I casually mentioned how much I loved treacle pudding, having encountered some in London. I was saying I wished I could make it but didn't know whether or not you could find treacle in America. A few months later the postman arrived with a large, leaking, and very sticky package. We peeled off the sodden wrapping paper to find two large cans of treacle, one blond and one dark. Up to that moment my only encounter with treacle, beyond the delectable pudding in London, was in *Oliver Twist*.

Well, now I knew it was as sticky as molasses. A considerable amount had dispensed itself throughout the government's mail en route, but after cleaning it all up we ended with two good-sized jars.

How to make treacle pudding I'd no notion at all. As I remembered, it was rather like cottage pudding, a sort of ambrosial cake with lemon sauce. I was always going to figure it out but never did. So the treacle followed us down here in the move from Connecticut to the Carolina mountains.

I descended to the cellar yesterday to search out my hooked-rug dyes so I could dye some more material. At Christmas I'd promised Joan that when I finished my current rug I'd make her one. She wants a rug like ours, flowers all over, called "Scattered posies" in the catalogue. I will make hers with a tan background. Ours has a white one but white would soil in New York City. So—down among the hooked-rug dye jars, in one of the two packages never yet opened since the move, there was the treacle that I'd forgotten all about. Now I will have to look up treacle pudding somewhere and experiment.

"What in the world does treacle taste like?" Bob asked, as we studied the glass jar with its thick dark contents. We opened and smelled it and concluded it was like molasses only more so!

I tucked it up on the top shelf, and now we shall see where we go from here.

Would it be good in bread in place of molasses? Best probably in treacle pudding.

The first crocuses are out, gold and bright as a sunbeam. Following them emerge the violet-blue and the white ones, also bordering the garden path. How cheery they all look—these earliest flowers. Of course, the January jasmine has been blooming happily for weeks and weeks, but a crocus is spring in essence, and a sweep of them in February is paradise indeed. The first florets in the blossom clusters of daphne odora are opening too. The fig tree is covered with fat green buds on three tall burgeoning stalks. And this morning a friend brought me two branches of flowering quince. They are so interestingly twisted and Japanese-looking, and the flowers are a kind of smoky rosy orange.

This afternoon our neighbor across the street was setting out crocuses that he'd bought in the fall and that had got tucked away out of sight and memory. They were all ready to bloom in the bag, so vitally alive was each bulb. Bob and I had wandered over to talk to him. Everywhere as far as we could see through the woods was daffodil greenery, six inches high and with buds, some even showing yellow.

Walking home, we examined ours along the fence. They were all up as were the wood hyacinths. The spring bulb pageant of Tryon begins this month and goes on almost till May.

High above these first spring flowers and appealing in their individual way are the seed pods on the giant tulip trees all around

Tryon. These pods were formed last fall and have actually been lovely all winter. They are a golden tan and spread over branches and twigs, each one a little sculptured tulip with petals slightly parted.

In Tryon spring comes slowly, a part of the town's unique charm. In New England spring holds back and then, all in a rush, is here, tumbling its treasures over the landscape at your feet. In a whisk it is gone.

In the South, where everything moves with a slower rhythm, the spirit of leisure prevails even in the gradual unfoldment of this well-loved season. We especially enjoy these long slow Southern springs, a little cold spell, a little warm spell, the latter increasing continually in predominance and length. And the first beginnings in February. Spring here is at least three months long and mounts in a crescendo till it breaks over the mountains and valleys in a tremendous flood of fragrance, color, and music. First of all along the marshes, streams and small lakes the alders stir and waken to toss their catkins in each passing zephyr. Tiny purple Carolina pine-sap flowers push up to loose their scent through the woods. The tops of the bare maple branches turn firey red. There seems a warm pinkish glow everywhere over all bare branches, brightening their hues.

I'm invariably surprised at the reaction of a friend when she hears that I've been sitting outdoors most of a February morning.

"Didn't you freeze? And what do you *do*? Just sitting! Aren't you bored?"

The answer to this is always no. I happen to like to " just sit."

Bob has long become accustomed to my predilection for this questionable pastime. On warmish days in fall or spring he may even join me for a little while. But he has never become as addicted as I.

This week has provided some lovely sunny days on our terrace, in a little spot where the wind is absent and the sun shines down. We have a chaise and cushions. Before settling, I wrap the car robe around me from back to front to keep out rear drafts. Thus bundled, I enjoy a couple of hours in the sun during the warmest part of the day. Possibly I will sew, or perhaps write letters, or read the current book, do the budget, pay bills. And always watch the birds come and go at the feeders. On days my fingers freeze, I wear wool mittens and read. Sometimes I just experience that enviable state of doing nothing and thinking nothing, a lovely interlude of merely being that sends me back into activities thoroughly refreshed.

I believe I have inherited the "sitting-out" habit! One of my earliest memories of my mother is the sight of her sitting in the pale winter sun in a little warm—well, reasonably warm at least—protected corner outside the house of my childhood. She would be reading or sewing or studying maps, which she loved. In the morning she would settle where the eastern sun streamed down upon her. At noon she would move to the south side of the house in another sheltered spot.

My mother would be wearing her old black sealskin coat, with a few rips in the pelt at the back where the sleeves were set in. As fast as one black sealskin coat wore out she bought another just like it, and the old one was relegated to "sitting out." Her hands would be in her black sealskin muff, and fur-lined velvet shoes would be keeping her size 3A feet warm. A toast-colored vicuna robe, bought on a trip to Peru with my father, was folded snugly around her.

In this household of my growing up, "sitting out" was an occupation in its own right, like knitting, or cooking, or reading, or taking a walk.

"What are you going to do this morning, Mame?" Aunt Alice would ask when she was visiting us.

"Well, Alice, I'm going to sit out. Won't you join me?"

Maybe Aunt Alice would or would not. Mostly she wouldn't, unless it was warm weather. In fact, in passing, she would glance out the window and shake her head as if my mother were slightly off her rocker as they said in those days. The river wind blowing right off chunks of ice that drifted down the Hudson River from Albany was kept off my staunch parent by the angles of the house. Some days, if it were warm enough, she might be hemstitching towels, or working on great needlepoint tapestry—which eventually covered a bench before the fireplace and is now a family heirloom.

Having inherited my mother's love for this pastime, it seems the most natural thing in the world for me to sit outdoors on sunny days almost all winter. There is something special about being outdoors with the cold, cold air on your face as you breathe. When you come in your skin glows and you feel a tingle. After I have been out an hour or two in that cold air, I always have a feeling of having encompassed a bit of all outdoors, and then I seem to bring it into the house with me. The sensation remains for several hours. Outside in the stillness of our winter woodland, I listen to the cardinal as it begins to sing more this month, if still hesitantly.

Perhaps it can't decide whether spring is really in the offing or not. The juncoes, a tufted titmouse or two, and some pine siskins in the bird feeders chirp to each other—and to me. I whistle back and they chirp in response. And we engage in some pleasant verbal communication in their language and my attempts at it.

When I sit there for a while the birds think I'm a piece of the house or perhaps some odd kind of bush that doesn't always stay rooted in one spot as a normal bush should. They become quite tame and come and go to the nearby feeders with the greatest nonchalance. On some days the chickadees gain the courage to light on the benches where I have my work. Politely they ask me in their language for sunflower seeds. I unwrap and go in for a handful. Now they light on my fingers and, taking one seed at a time, fly up onto a maple branch to crack and eat it. Then they return, darting in little scallops, for another. A whole flock of six or seven may be in the Southern magnolia branches at once, and coming in turn to me for seed. But if there is anything left in the feeders they consider me that strange bush and don't come near.

Regular bird seed found in the markets has in it some varieties that the birds don't much care for. It may be the wheat germ or cod liver oil. Anyway, they leave it until last. First of all the sunflower seeds disappear, and this is why they welcome me with an extra cache of them in my pockets.

On Valentine's Day Bob brought me a package of Tootsie Rolls. Upon rare occasions he brings me these delectable and sinister confections. When I was a child they were one of my favorite things. I used to save my allowance, and some of the newspaper and candy stores on Fifty-ninth Street were haunted by me and my friends. I commuted from Spuyten Duyvil to the Brearley School when it was on Sixty-first Street. Sometimes I would stay in town for the afternoon and night with Hoppy, one of my contemporaries, and we would go to a movie at the old Plaza Theater when it was on Fifty-ninth Street and less elegant than today. Settled in the dark theater watching some bloodcurdling love tale were two stringy thirteen-year-olds munching Tootsie Rolls. Neither the movies nor the Tootsie Rolls were forbidden but were mildly frowned upon by our elders.

When Bob brings me a Tootsie Roll today and I savor that delicious chocolatey sweetness and its gummy consistancy, for a split moment I slip back to special afternoons fraught with adventure— buying rice cakes in a little Japanese store, to conceal in our beds until the moment when the lights were turned out; hovering in a small cobwebby pet shop buying chameleons, and mealworms to feed them —to Hoppy's mother's horror. Or acquiring telescope-eyed fan-tailed goldfish to be carried home in leaky little cartons with a whisk of greenery for their health. With what harmless delight did all these things fill school afternoons.

The Tootsie Rolls available today actually have thinned out considerably, and changed not only in price but shape, and even the flavor seems rather less glamorous. But no matter, on Valentine's Day or some occasion when Bob brings me a package they still evoke memories and for this I love them, and him for remembering.

Many of our sturdiest roots stretch back into childhood. Much of what we are today had its beginnings way back then. Intermittent glimpses of what *was* often help us to understand better what is.

Besides, I like trips to anywhere, and slipping backward is a favorite journey.

Recently a nondomestic friend of mine was admiring my hooked rug so nearly completed.

"It must take a lot of patience," she said, "to make a rug like that."

At her words I was reminded of the story of a certain Japanese gardener of the old school. The man worked silently and methodically and for long minutes over a bonsai. Finally, a visitor said, "You must need a lot of patience to do that." "Oh, no," he replied promptly, "patience is needed only when you are doing something you do not like." How much wisdom comes to us from the East.

I was sitting in our living room watching the birds darting from tree to bird feeder to bush to fence and back to the suet basket, the latter being high on the trunk of an oak, high as we can reach. We have to keep in mind the neighborhood dogs, who would love nothing better than to get at it. This morning there were several pairs of lovely purple finches in the oak. The gentleman looks for all the world as if he'd been loosed in a patch of ripe strawberries and had wallowed. He fills the garden with his brilliant tint; and now a pair of cardinals arrived—like streaks of fire through the woods, and always a decorative note. Several little goldfinches and nuthatches were flitting about the suet. The Carolina wren joined them. He is a delicious chocolate brown and so bright and perky.

All at once I held my breath—there he came—the pileated woodpecker. The great bird is a dramatic creature and fascinating to watch. First you hear his rather raucous tone as he announces himself from a little way off. He lit on the back side of the oak. Gradually he inched his way around to the front, where the suet was, and where I could see him. I sat completely still, hardly daring to breathe. After much looking over his shoulder with each move closer to be sure no danger lurked, he finally settled close to the suet holder. He was now able to reach his long sharp black beak through the wire netting. His brilliant red crest was plainly visible. What an enormous bird he is, with such great feet and claws. He ate and ate and no other bird came near while he was there.

A car drove past on the street. He hardly paused. But when Bob, coming back with the mail, turned in the drive, the enormous bird took fright and flew off. But he is still there, built into my memory, and at will I can recall the sight of him.

He goes into my memory file. Betty has just introduced me to the joys of a memory file. She has developed a habit of building in mental images of certain places, experiences, sights, things she loves. At will, then, in waiting moments, in bed at night if wakeful, or any time at all, she takes these out of her memory file and relives them.

What a wonderful custom. I have already started my memory file with this moment.

Betty and I have a wonderful exchange that goes on by phone more or less any time. When one of us finds a quote we especially like, we call and share it with the other. Hers to me this morning is one of my favorites.

"Be like the bird that, lighting on a branch too slight, feels it give way beneath her and sings, knowing she hath wings."

"No author known," said Betty. What a lovely thing to ponder.

"No encounter with a being or thing in the course of our life lacks hidden significance. The highest culture of the soul remains basically arid and barren unless day by day, waters of life pour into the soul from those little encounters to which we give their due." There is a lifetime of wisdom to contemplate in these words of Martin Buber. It seems to me accumulating memories and reliving them is rather a wonderful way of letting "the waters of life" pour into our spirits.

While adding new inward cargo I find it also useful to reevaluate other inward cargo and see what I may be carrying that I no longer have need of and would like to drop off.

The early part of the year seems an appropriate time to clean and sort out not only cupboards but my thinking as well.

How can I take on the new unless there is space? Therefore I must dispense with what I no longer need in attitudes and points of view as well as possessions. Just as surely as those chairs, sofas, beds, books, are ours, equally so are certain ways of thinking. And the question arises: What do I want in this particular phase of living? I scrutinize carefully my habitual way of approaching situations and habits of thought and give them all a sorting out and eliminating.

This is very easy to say but it is not at all easy to do. Often I find myself responding to specific occurrences in the same manner—and perhaps not always a very good one—as of ten years ago! Now I would like to shed that method of response and create a new one, one more in keeping with my life today and the era of the moment. Step one is at least recognizing what is surplus and needs altering and making the effort to change.

During any month of the year we have days when we feel as though a pile of books, topped by two flatirons, were pressing down our spirits. These are the times to draw from our deeper selves the particular things that we each have in the way of spirit raisers. Some of the special moments that one has stored away can now be a large help. If we can somehow catch a moment of low ebb before it gets too well entrenched or puts down roots, we can much more readily raise it.

Cleaning drawers and cupboards often lifts my spirits. To neaten something outward seems to bring some order to my inward self. I gain a degree of balance in my thinking that often points to the next step to take in the dilemma—be it an outward one or an inward one.

Occasionally we feel that certain situations in our lives must be radically changed for us to move forward. At such times I often find that while a visible change may be needed, even more pertinent and vital is the need to change my thinking. Miracles of change first happen in the inward realm. Subsequently the inner emerges to be reflected in the outer.

I wonder if we don't all have times when we simply cannot get our spirits off the ground, when they sink into a muddy puddle and remain there. I know I do. In these gloomy interludes I cannot and don't even want to try to lift my thinking. At such moments I am unable to think clearly, only to feel, and I feel terrible. This I have discovered is the time for pure holding. Just hold—and my best way to hold is to do something for someone else. Another way I have of holding is to tackle a project around home that I've been putting off for weeks. One of my wise friends always says that when upset about anything the thing to do is to "act instead of reacting." That simple statement has often lifted me out of the doldrums.

I have one or two friends to whom I often turn when I'm in a low mood. Sharing my temporary low moment with them I feel much better. I've got the trouble off my shoulders and have accepted their warm concern and understanding. This all helps. It's also rewarding to share a high moment with a close friend. If I share this in some way by doing something special for my friend, the high moment rises twice as high.

Friendship I often see as composed of three circles. We all have at least one person, perhaps two or three, with whom we share in depth, one we can completely trust and who trusts us. This is the inside circle. Surrounding this is a second circle, including friends whom we value but never share with on a very deep level. With these we may spend many pleasant creative hours, discussing ideas, and engaging in interesting activities together. Outside this is a large circle of acquaintances. Sad are the periods in our lives when we find ourselves spending a disproportionate amount of time and energy in this outer circle at the expense of the inner ones. The outermost circle, the peripheral one, has its value, its casual joys. But these mere brief contacts at a meeting, or concert or lecture, where greetings are warm but nothing of real significance is exchanged, are poor fare unless some of the other relationships are added. For the greatest sense of fulfillment, I find myself slipping from one to the other throughout my days.

A fire glowed in the fireplace, a slim stick of sandlewood incense sent up a winding curl of blue smoke. Banks, a good friend of mine, and I were both spread out in her living room surrounded by skeins of wool. She was teaching me to crochet. I was deep in a new world—chain stitches, single crochets, double crochets, standards, shells. Each craft, I find, has its own language. We had a Bucilla loom, a small plastic affair with a number of pegs in it. Following specific directions, you wound the wool round and about here and there and in a few minutes you had a beguiling fluffy wool flower. When you had accumulated a whole pile of these, you crocheted them together and had an afghan, a sweater, a cap, a bed jacket—anything you liked. We kept poring through *Woman's Day* and *Family Circle*, looking up the rules and experimenting with a variety of colors and weights of wool. Outside it was cold and rainy, and what could be more fun than this? Our imagination soared miles ahead of our small loom and crochet hook, envisioning great productions for family birthdays and Christmases ahead.

After a while we paused and sipped sassafras tea and Banks told me about Aunt Charity Bradley who lives in Mill Spring and makes patchwork quilts. And now we are miles ahead down *that* lane by making mental patchwork quilts. Patchwork quilts are a good project and I've a large box filled with patches in tiny gay prints and large square pieces of new material in a vast variety of gay colors.

There is so much pleasure and companionship in handwork. Banks loves it as much as I do and we are both brimful of ideas and plans. Good thing it's mid-winter because this is the ideal time to follow at least some of these many enchanted directions that present themselves. Last week Bob and I went to Spartanburg where I lost myself for an hour in the Knitting Nook. That's where I got the little flower looms. The two women who run it are friendly and cooperative and they sent me home with all kinds of wools in marvelous colors and said after I had a stack of flowers made to come back and they'd teach me how to crochet them together.

As February draws to a close the first daffodils are out, everywhere through gardens and woods. In our woodland glade we've several hundred of the little low-growing early ones with yellow trumpets. You see them when driving over back roads where stark chimneys of burned-out cabins still stand. They have escaped and spread abundantly in this whole area. Everyone who gardens grows them and shares. Also gay in the garden is our Oregon grape, tossing gold tassels over spiney green leaves, while the andromeda by the front door hangs out its fringe of snowy tassels.

Today it's misty, hazy, rainy and cold outside, in the forties at four o'clock. The garden is gray, the terrace bricks are shiny wet, and the fence is streaked with water forming interesting patterns on the pickets. Sitting before my hooking frame I was arranging the colors for the new rug I'm about to start. First of all, Bob lit a fire. Then I heard a stirring about in the

51

kitchen. Presently he appeared with a tea tray—our little Japanese teapot and two cups and a plate of crackers frosted with something delicious.

The fire today is one of Bob's masterpieces; it goes on and on with never a hesitation after the first match. We are warm and cozy here indoors, sipping peppermint tea and munching the slightly sweet crackers. I turn to my other rug, completed and waiting for me to do the hem around. It's going to look wonderful in this room in front of the fireplace. The strands of many-colored wool hanging beside me ready for the next rug are decorative and an invitation to begin. The Christmas poinsettia is still beautiful, and bright and gay as Christmas week. The little brass incense burner sparkles in the firelight. The colors of the room in the gathering dusk and the glow of the flames are muted. The terrarium beside me is green and gay with red berries and new uncurling ferns. I am memorizing this moment. The sound, the fragrance of peppermint tea, the aroma of wood burning in the grate, the comfortable ticking of the cuckoo clock, both of us here together exchanging ordinary everyday thoughts, just being ourselves, easy, relaxed, content.

This is a special memory for the file—to draw out and relive when I need it.

3

March is a Time of Response

A LOVELY soft but definite spring rain has been falling all night. A good sound to sleep by, especially since it gives a new tone to the music of the running brook. And then by morning it stopped and the sun emerged. The mountains are again raspberry tipped as the first rays paint them. Along branches and twigs everywhere a million sparkles of glinting rainbows swing in all the waterdrops, turning our woodland to fairyland.

In the garden daphne odora is opening flower clusters, each one a little snowball of fragrance. Some full-out purple crocuses that lay right down in last night's rain are making an effort to lift themselves, and are already partway up. The cone-shaped first hyacinth greenery is emerging from the earth a little more each day. The drifts of myrtle turn bluer with more blossoms opening every hour. How amazing is clematis: the stalk from the ground up grows lean and lank and ineffective looking. But three feet higher a shower of foliage develops. New leaves have grown greener and larger since last night's rain, and many long slim flower buds perch along the topmost runners.

Everywhere birds are singing, differently and more continuously than last month. These days we sense that they are busy about their own private concerns. Their songs have become a question and response. You hear the cardinal way off to the right somewhere. "Springtime, springtime, springtime?" he chants, his trilling notes rising at the end like a question. From high up in a different tree, but not too far away, comes the answering call of his mate. And so with all the birds —there seems to be a twosome quality in their singing.

I saw him then, the first butterfly. He is violet and fragile, a mere breath of life but life and vitality all the same. This ephemeral creature of grace and delicacy drifts about in free swoops and curves. For several moments I pause, silent and still, watching him. Can I feel with him a little of what he might feel, of sunlight on soft violet wings, of a whole fresh world of spring to explore?

This small life is one to revere and respect. A tramp from a careless foot could extinguish the tiny creature, but no, he lives, and rises from where he is poised on a daphne floret to float up over the fence and away on butterfly business, far off in another dimension of existence.

Alone in the garden sharing these few moments with my winged friend I have felt strangely close to him. He and I have together been a part of the beginnings of a new season, of a new day. The morning is the richer for me because this small butterfly passed my way.

March here in our mountains is beauty everywhere and emerging growth, with nature on all sides the continuous giver. Up the valleys and through the coves, along roadsides and sweeping over mountain slopes is such beauty we can hardly take it in. Nature now gives us the first redbud and the beginnings of the dogwood. Each day and each hour seem to unfold further.

The lavender mistiness of the redbud comes first while the dogwood is still budding. Everywhere stands trillium, with patterned leaves and dark red flowers. Tiny blue hepaticas must be sought out in sheltered glens, where you pause and part the leaves on the forest floor. There you discover small wide-eyed blue flowers and furry heart-shaped leaves. The miniature white feathery blooms of the rue anemone are like snowflakes dropped over the red-brown pine needles.

Bloodroot stands prim and white on the woodland floor, each many-petaled flower crisp and cool and fresh as the morning dew, and with a tufted gold center. You have to pause in silence or, better yet, kneel down before one of these small wild beauties to drink in the wonder of it. You study how the flower is made, how it emerges from the earth a solitary folded blossom. Then you watch the petals open. Each bloom is followed by a slim pointed green seed pod and then there emerges from the ground a single, deeply indented leaf standing on end like a small Japanese fan.

We hear about something called "Earth Shine" these days. Here in our mountains we have observed an equally exciting kind of shine—woods shine, forest shine.

All winter, until new foliage emerges, you see everywhere a truly glorious woodland glow. Laurel, holly, rhododendron, pines, Southern magnolia, leucothoe, English ivy trailing up trees, and, down among the leaves, galax foliage, along with countless other creeping and growing things, all catch the sun on their evergreen foliage. Greenery everywhere catches these beams of light, sifting down through bare branches, and reflects back to us a vivid sparkle—a woods shine.

The whole forest is vibrantly alive with this shimmering and constantly changing light during the winter months. Walking over the trails and living surrounded by the woods, we find ourselves immersed in it, bathed in it, whenever the sun is out.

Looking straight at the sun for more than a split second would blind us, but we can readily respond to its streamers of reflected light. The great forces of nature are almost beyond our direct comprehension. Who can completely understand the magnitude of wind, for example? Yet when we see a blade of grass bending to its gentle blow, or sturdy pine trees swaying against the stars at night, in these small evidences we touch a vast and changeable power.

And rain, an incomprehensible force perhaps, but one that reaches us when we watch a few drops falling on a brick terrace or listen to the patter on leaves at night.

Oceans, tides, rivers, lakes and their ways are great mysteries almost beyond understanding. But we can relate to a small brook, moss bordered, flowing at our feet.

Thus in small portions does much of the beauty and wonder of the earth reach through to us. Life, knowing our capabilities and limitations, shares its miracles indirectly and a little at a time according to our ability to take in.

How often I need to remind myself to trust life in the way it gives, and to let it funnel into me not only through the simple and moving experiences of nature that vary with every season, but also through other means—through our fellow man, words spoken, in what we read, in the ideas and inspirations that come to mind and spirit. If we are alert and listening and are able to receive the messages of life when they are first gently given, we learn and grow with the least wear and tear!

It's eight-thirty in the morning and, with the top down, we're coasting along over the countryside toward Charlotte. Spring is flinging her earliest colors and her delicate gentleness through field and meadow. A light brush of green tangles in bare branches of trees along roadside and woodlands. This morning the air is soft and the sky and mountains a sort of violet-grayblue. Against this background great peach orchards fling their Valentine-pink blossoms over the land-scape. We are in the midst of a foam of pink as feathery flowers, as far as we can see, toss themselves over light gray branches. Everywhere beneath is a carpet of orange-red earth. There are still many tight buds yet to unfold along the twigs.

When we come to a particularly appealing hillside of trees, we stop the car and get out to walk through them.

"Oh, look," I exclaimed, seeing a great branch broken off, lying on the ground but still budding and partly in bloom. "We can pick *these*." Naturally we'd never dream of picking any from the trees.

"Oh, no," said Bob, who hates to dampen my enthusiasm but is also very law-abiding."How would people seeing us with armfuls of peach blossoms know we had picked from fallen branches?"

"Oh, hum, I suppose you're right," I agreed sadly. I probably would end up in jail if I didn't have Bob now and then gently reminding me of laws and ethics. No matter, we can simply take the wonder of these blooms home in memory—that way they never wilt and we always have them!

Wandering up the slight rise and through the rows of trees we kept gaining height. Turning about suddenly we caught the view of acres and acres of trees in full bloom on the level below us. Nothing could ever be more meltingly beautiful than these undulating sheets of pink stretching toward the horizon.

A friend of ours said recently, "You have to think about *something* when you first wake up, so why not choose something serene and beautiful?" This was his form of morning meditation. These peach orchards as they are this morning I can never forget. They shall reside in my memory file of wonderful moments to keep for when needed.

After lunch we found ourselves out in a churchyard next to Ivey's where we had stopped. We sat watching the spray from a fountain rise up and spill down. A fountain is something alive, and I love watching the water spurt up from each jet. At the top drops seem to balance in midair a moment before falling. Somewhere in a treetop a mockingbird was singing. Children's voices in the distance drifted our way, and presently a mother and three little girls passed by. The children bent to examine some white stars of Bethlehem. Each blossom is exquisite, six petals, two tiers of three petals each.

We drove home filled with peace and contentment, and silent a good part of the way. The peaches in the afternoon light were equally beautiful and breathtaking. Here and there in the woods along the highway the sun filtered through the trees, touching new moss and tinting it a vivid, golden chartreuse. In a field were half a dozen chestnut-brown horses grazing, their coats winter-long and shaggy. Back-lit as they were, each had a golden aura outlining his shape. Beyond the horses were forsythia bushes full out, fountains of gold, also back-lit and dazzling.

We could each feel in the other a sense of joy and serenity, and to a degree that no words were necessary. Sometimes you want to share in words new or sudden beauty, excitement, insights and fresh experiences. But often two people who are close do not want or need words. The response and sharing from one to the other is better in silence. So it was this day.

With the top still down we arrived home, so full of sunshine and air I hardly remember eating supper and I think we were both sound asleep by eight.

Next morning by seven-thirty I was dressed and out in the garden, clearing leaves away from the primroses and feeding them. We have seven healthy plants all in bud along the garden path. These represent about three dozen bought and set out. The others succumbed to mysterious creatures—pine mice? moles? snails? Who knows, but we treasure these vigorous seven so alive and thriving and covered with buds. The blue one was the first to open. Nearby are yellows also out. Each blossom in a cluster of many is nearly two inches across. I was appreciating the primroses when all of a sudden I beheld a snail. An enemy! I don't like to do what I must do but snails love these plants and eat their leaves like lettuce. My reverence for life means I revere the life of a primrose more than that of the snail. Therefore I squash each one as found, every time with a small apology, because after all they have their place. Actually, they are charming to look at, two little horns out ahead as they slide curiously over a rock, carrying their homes on their backs. But so there—I demolish another!

Just across the path the bloodroot, in bud when I first went out, was opening while I worked around, a little wider each time I looked. Pink-tipped arbutus flowers were also abundant. Six Kaufmanniana tulip buds (the water-lily tulip) are slim and pointed, a glorious carmine-rose hue.

I began digging up green rosettes of ajuga that were crowding the arbutus. Neighbors were coming to get it this morning. How good it felt, kneeling on the earth, plant food in a plastic pail beside me, small basket of hand tools also close, and birds singing in the oak above. Every time I looked up the foliage appeared to be more out, and the dusting of green over bare branches ever greener. Some tree buds are chartreuse, some a vivid spring green, while the maples are red as could be.

At this moment six hyacinths at the entrance to the garden path are in full, full bloom. The sun shining on them seems to draw out their fragrance. Actually I smell them as I open the front door, but when lying on the garden bench looking down at them the scent rises up all around and I am in a world of hyacinths. When you smell a flower you enter, for the moment, a world completely undefined, a world where thinking, reasoning, logic and material things do not exist, a world boundless and open-ended. To some people such areas of being are almost closed, or perhaps never have been opened, touched, explored. Mostly we live in a thinking world where knowledge and material things are the basis of our activities and culture. It is good to be aware that the two kinds of existence, the material and the nonmaterial, occur side by side. It is refreshing to slip from one way of being into the other, from the thinking into the nonthinking by the simple route of smelling a hyacinth on a sunny morning.

I look at the detail of a floret, the beautiful glossy reflexing petals, the shine on each one, a shine of satin it is. I touch them; the firmness of the flower against my finger gives a sense of the vigor and vitality of the plant.

A garden is yesterday, today and tomorrow. These hyacinths are yesterday, today and tomorrow all in the moment of now. I feel again the pleasure of planting them last fall, loosening the soil and settling the fat round bulbs down under. I am remembering how all winter I enjoyed knowing they were there.

We watched them come up a week or so ago. First the pointed cone of bright green through the warming earth; then the cone parts and the buds, tight and green-white, emerge and open more each day. Now a hyacinth from each bulb is full out, and down by the base of its stalk in the heart of the foliage is a second bloom waiting to open.

The trailing arbutus is blooming, sweet

scented and a delight. The little pool is mossy on one side—with iris on the other side sending up charming green spears, and full of promise. The Burford holly is humming with bees. The holly will have a bumper crop of berries this fall, for all the bushes are covered with buds and flowers and everywhere there is the music of bees.

The whole garden path is aglow with flowers and promises. Lemon mint is fresh and pungent. Columbine sends up flower stalks; Virginia bluebells too. The scattering of columbine seeds that Betty gave me last fall are all up several inches.

Out here with nature exploding on every side I can almost hear the sap rising in flower, bush and tree, in garden and woodland, and also in myself. In a garden in the spring it's easy to feel and identify with this life-giving upward flow of sap. Perhaps we all have a kind of "sap" that rises at this time of year, sending through us a sense of special energy. Sometimes it seems almost in the form of music. Something within me beats with a new rhythm and sings along with the birds overhead. Something that soon melts into the broader enveloping symphony of spring.

Late yesterday afternoon Bob and I set forth, with trowels and two plastic pails, to go up the mountain to a woodland area where the bulldozers will presently be running, to dig up bloodroot. Surely we're doing nature a favor to bring back as many of these wild plants as possible to preserve in the garden before the proposed roads are built.

What a beautiful time I had, down among the leaves with my hands in the rich black soil, wiggling the trowel around to loosen the bloodroot. Now and again, looking across through the woods, I saw Bob bent over filling his pail with bloodroot plants. The bloodroot is a kind of knobby business that runs on and on with a bunch of root hairs at the base of the stem. You are bound to cut the root but it doesn't really matter. Where the trowel cleanly shaves it, a vivid red surface is bared. You may have wondered why this pure-white flower with a chaste gold-tufted center is given such a lurid name. But when you dig it up in the woods you know. We drifted home at dusk, car top down, with two pails of plants.

How good to be out in the crisp early-morning air setting out these interesting little plants. I was arranging them along the garden path. Some of these spring mornings it's hard to wait to get dressed before going outdoors. I don't even try, but go out in robe and slippers. And now, with all the plants snug in place, the imminent rain will settle and refresh them and they will scarcely know they have been moved. It rains sixty inches in a year here. There is seldom a drought to worry about.

On a recent sunny morning Bob and I found ourselves out in the garden pulling up onion grass. Onion grass is a delightful shade of blue-green, and beautiful with tall slim streamers of foliage. How readily it comes up after a rain. We're also tying up the vines on the fence. Bob stands on one side and I on the other while we pass green string back and forth through the quarter-inch spaces between pickets. Clematis, jessamine, roses and ivy all need tying.

In spring the great exchange begins, the exchange between man and nature. We take action, we give, and plants promptly respond. A few days after we had tied up the small ivy tendrils they were clinging, on their own, to the wooden fence. Everywhere we shape and prune more blooms and beauty result. We feed the daffodils each year and they respond by giving us larger and lusher blooms. In gardening the more we give the more we receive. This two-way communication relates us to elements beyond our house walls in such a satisfying way and enables us to feel a part of the growing world.

Whether in the garden or the house, in relationships or activities, we always have something to give to living. Life responds through the same or different channels, and we receive in more ways than we can ever reckon, or could have given!

What is so irresistible about shells on the beach? We were strolling along the warm white sand and here was a shell I must pick up, and there another. Each is beautiful, exquisite in pattern, shape, color, contour, texture.

We are shell collectors in only a very small way. On any beach we find ourselves exploring we always have to pick up a few. At home I arrange them on a shelf, rather casually sending some off to the grandchildren and sharing them with anyone who wants a few.

Here we were at Sanibel Island, spending an idyllic week at Island Inn, right on the beach. Our room and balcony looked out into a seagrape tree and, beyond cocoanut trees, to the blue gulf. We heard the waves breaking as we fell asleep. We were that near. We didn't come in our tent-trailer this time because we wanted to experience the enchantment of the inn.

I wonder if it's the do-nothing aspect of shell collecting that makes it such an engaging pastime. There surely is a fascination about it all. Often we say let's not bother this time. But both Bob and I are incapable of walking along the sand without looking down and, once you look down, this bit of dried stringy seaweed in a dusty-coral tone, and that small spiral shell, prove a strong invitation and one I cannot refuse. Outside each bedroom door on the porch is a little table where people arrange their shells. Our table gradually filled up with what had proved irresistible.

Often that week we sat on the beach for hours—never tiring as we watched the pelicans fly by. They swoop so low over the surface that their wings seem merely a few hair-widths above the water. I can never watch a pelican without smiling. They seem to me such amusing creatures. Hundreds of gulls always gathered on the sand, or skimmed the water, and they would let you come close. Last night we walked along the beach into a flaming sunset. What a beautiful contrast to the perpendiculars of our own pines and mountains is this broad and vast expanse of sea and sky and orange-sunset colors merging one into another.

We are collecting ways of doing nothing and places to do it in. This is one of the best, lying on the beach, listening to the rhythm of the waves and the high, thin call of an occasional bird.

Each afternoon about five we drive over to the Sanibel bird sanctuary to watch flocks of roseate spoonbills come in for the night. With the glasses we admire the pink flamingoes, the anhinga bird, and the innumerable herons and egrets. Among the most exciting of all the birds are the skimmers, with their large, long, vivid-orange beaks and feet. They stand in flocks on the inlet shore all facing in one direction, quiet, colorful, and dignified. And then displaying streaks of dazzling tones they take off in a group.

What an important part chance plays in our lives. Because you took this road instead of that one, or chose this kind of holiday instead of that, forces were started at work in your experience, lines of thinking, personal contacts, and friends who will play a vital part in your future. If you had taken the other road instead it would have all been different. How did you happen to meet your husband, for example? In my own case, it was because I played tennis one day in a certain place and met someone who very much intrigued me. Suppose I'd played tennis in a different place, or had been away on a visit that week? What then?

Bob has often ruminated on the chance remark of a college roommate that led him to follow up on a job opening in New York City. A different chance remark might just as well have led him to a job in Boston or Chicago and we never would have met.

Look back through your life, choose some of the most important aspects of it, and you may be astonished to realize how often chance has led you. This all suggests to me how extremely important it is not to have one's life all blocked out, not to have the days and weeks totally organized. I think it's essential to leave gaps and interludes for spontaneous action, for it is often in spontaneity and surprises that we open ourselves to the unlimited opportunities and new areas brought into our lives by chance. It is often in consequence of these very moments that our life paths take their most interesting turnings.

Actually there are two ways of opening ourselves to chance. Besides leaving gaps and interludes there is the need to be curious, alert, ready, open; to be willing and interested to look out a new window and sometimes to listen and take in completely new thoughts; to step through an unfamiliar doorway; to explore an untried path or highway.

I was sitting on a bank picking violets. What a marvelous deep purple shade they were. Among them, and in contrast, were a few of the lighter two-toned Confederate violets. I was picking some of each and some of the lovely heart-shaped green leaves too. Birds were singing and overhead were sweeps of pure-white dogwood, and new leaves unfolding in the trees in all their spring hues.

The simple occupations often bring the greatest pleasures. So it was that morning. I was sliding my fingers down along one crisp green stem after another to get each as long as possible. How lovely was my handful of shiny peppermint green stems.

One flower here, one there, as I moved slowly along the bank. Now I settled down, surrounded by violets to pick in one place for a while. Off in the distance I could hear cars streaming past on the highway, each going its own way, following its own direction, achieving, doing, accomplishing. All to the good, to be sure, but my moments in that bed of violets I would trade with no one.

You cannot hurry when you pick violets. You choose one here, another there, constantly making decisions. This one is such a beauty and that one I cannot leave. A gentle pastime!

I remember as a child one of the earliest springtime pleasures was going out with one or two of my friends to pick violets. We children had a number of private secret places. We would whisper to each other at recess about whether the time had come to go that afternoon. Was it a little early? We would go and see anyway. Early spring was also pollywog time. We used to get jars of these small dark wiggly creatures. We'd watch them turn to miniature frogs in our rooms and then loose them back in their stream.

Picking violets when I was a child marked the official end of winter, the turn of the season when a new face of nature became visible. Gathering these spring harbingers were moments to treasure; so was giving them in small tight bouquets to mother or father, a favorite aunt, or my sisters. I would surprise them with my bouquets on their dressers or beside their beds. A particularly warm smile of thanks, an appreciative arm around, a hug, and something good flowed through to me. And then there came the time when our own children would bring us small bunches of violets on those first days of spring. And how I loved to come in at the end of the day from shopping, gardening or visiting to find these evidences of affection in our room.

Picking violets travels down through the generations. These days our grandchildren bring in tight handfuls of purple beauties.

Gathering violets now still gives me a feeling of deep content. It can be a time almost of meditation while choice and secret feelings surface.

Anne Lindbergh writes, "When the mind is left to its ponderings it brings up its own treasures of the deep."

4

April Is Easter in Nature

THE whole world is shiny bright with fresh spring newness. What is more appealing than tiny new unfolding fig leaves? The chartreuse greenness of them! The defined pattern and ribbing on the back of each one! And finally and best of all the tender little just-born figs clinging to the bare stalk. It's as if in their eagerness for life these small fruits could not wait for the tree to be fully clothed before emerging into being. How different is the young foliage on every tree, the oak from the maple, the sourwood from the sassafras. And there are no beginning leaves more intriguing than those of the tulip tree.

The clean newness of the world everywhere inspires us to freshen up inside the house too. I must get some material to recover the hassock and shouldn't we brighten up the living-room chairs? Those covers have been on for twenty years and lasted wonderfully, to be sure, but there comes a time when you want colors different, more vivid, or in some way altered. This was brought on by the recently completed hooked rug laid down before the fireplace. Its gay tones make the chairs appear dull. One thing is leading to another, I can see!

But it's difficult to stay outdoors even to think of pretty materials. April is delirious, mad, marvelous, and enchanting with touches of new outdoor magic every hour.

Gradually, due to a constantly growing bright tangle of beginning leaves on all the trees, we are losing our mountain views, but the nearby scenes are breathtaking so we cannot care less. Climbing high in the sourwood across the street our neighbor's wisteria is spilling its first lavender blooms and the sweet fragrance floats through the air. Later, wisteria petals will fall like violet snow over us and our terrace, but now they are just coming out.

The blue spires of our ajuga flowers were never lusher or more flourishing. They are hosts to myriads of bumblebees during the warm noontime. These marvelous bees are the ones that aerodynamically cannot fly.

According to their weight and shape and size of wing it is said to be impossible for a bumblebee to take off. I pause to watch these impossibilities here on our place and consider how in all fields of living the impossible frequently occurs. It stretches our horizons in a healthy manner to recognize aspects of life and events that cannot be measured and accounted for and explained, that just occur, breaking all laws. This gives a good feeling that anything can happen; a feeling that I like to live with.

Along the garden path azaleas are taking the lead in the pageant of the month, more blossoms emerging each day. In all stages they are superb. I love the pointed buds, tipped in color, the first ones opening. When fully out, the bush is quite hidden by flowers. We have azaleas in white, pink, scarlet, salmon, a delicate orchid tone, and some whites that are casually dusted with pink. Together they create a magnificent show.

Last month in March spring was new, and a beautiful surprise every day. In its earliest beginnings there is a tentative, unreal quality about this season. Spring is hesitant, unsure, here today and gone tomorrow. But now in April it's real. It is here, it is now. We accept its glory and authority.

The temperature may drop to the high thirties on some nights, but we know spring will not retreat and we are in the heart and the very wonder of it. Each year I think I remember, but never truly can, the particular and intimate beauty of our small garden when all the spring flowers are out. Not only is our own garden sensational, but so are all the gardens and the whole countryside.

It is Eastertime in nature and I feel its stirrings. I begin to sense in my thinking and my feeling the same creative expansiveness that we are surrounded by outdoors. The oak tree is pushing off dead leaves in order to send out this year's buds and foliage, and thus to fulfill itself. May I likewise free myself for greater fulfillment. May I identify with nature and reflect fresh vigor in all the areas of thinking, being, and doing. This becomes my Easter prayer.

Some people's best ideas come at midnight but mine wake me with the dawn. So it was this morning. Before I knew who I was, where, why, or what day it was, I had an insistant urge to grow a small salad garden. When we moved here we chose a woodland glade. We had decided that, while we had raised our own vegetables for many years and loved having them, all good things and people come to a turn in the road and maybe we had arrived at such a one and should transfer our energies to other areas.

We both had missed our vegetable garden, but more or less secretly, being loyal to a mutual decision. Also, we could buy Mrs. Jennings's home-grown produce which sustained us and prevented our being too nostalgic.

When Bob got up I was standing in the bathroom, gazing rapturously out the window at a section of our woodland, a small sunny clearing. I was studying the lay of the land. With all our beloved trees we are short of sun but there is this one little area. Looking out and envisioning a few vegetables was exciting. I could imagine a minigarden with lots of topsoil and fertilizer so it would yield richly.

"Do you think maybe we should grow

some tomatoes out there?" I asked Bob before he was very awake.

He looked over my shoulder vaguely.

"Do you think we could?" he asked, dreamily. And then he suddenly seemed to wake up. "You know, I do believe we could!"

The sun was streaming down in that small spot. Later in the morning we were walking past Cowan's hardware store. There on the sidewalk outside were flats of flourishing little tomato plants. We stopped. I bent over and touched the leaves and then smelled my fingers. That wonderful tomato fragrance! We drove home with three Big Boy tomatoes, two yellow ones and one tiny red cherry tomato clustered around my feet. Bob filled the wheelbarrow with sand, soil, and sawdust and began turning over the earth. Next he added cottonseed meal and ashes from the fireplace and mixed it all in. This is the most minigarden we ever had. It is about three by six—a token garden, but a garden none the less.

These days when you buy seedlings in peat pots they never wilt after being set out. Bob got two cucumber plants in

Landrum for our "farm" but alas, we can't find any lettuces. Everyone says it's too late —not to plant seed but to buy seedlings. So we got a package of Black Seeded Simpson, a package of Salad Bowl and one of Boston. Bob sowed a six-inch row of each. Nothing is more delectable than home-grown lettuces!

We had no sooner got the garden this far when, like a magnet, it began drawing plants from friends. A fabulous Australian onion, whatever that is, from Gladys; a root of the herb comfrey from Horace. A little pot of parsley subsequently appeared and some tiny basil seedlings. And Banks brought over a pot of sage.

"No man must plant or have anything to do with this plant," she said, laughing. "Bad luck if he does."

I quickly looked up "sage" and discovered some further fascinating lore about it.

A person never dies while the sage is flourishing in his garden!

> He that would live for aye
> Must eat sage in May.

Sage keeps you not only alive but young forever (so said the ancients) and filled with vim and energy. It clears the mind and restores the memory. Chop it up in bread-and-butter sandwiches. The doctors of the Middle Ages used it to cure just about anything from a sore throat to rheumatism. And it also alleviates grief! Sage tea is a favorite in China, and sage honey is a luxury.

Banks, I can see, gave me not a plant, but a way of life.

I set it out in the "farm" today.

Lending a jaunty note to this area are five six-foot tomato stakes. Bob cut them on the hillside and they have a rustic, rakish, and informal look as they angle off in different directions. He also made a wattle cucumber fence out of prunings from the crab apple tree. It has an appealing hand-crafted look and makes me feel that Snow White and the Seven Dwarfs must live just over the hill.

Thus our salad garden, that was not even an idea last week, has been born.

All gardeners love watching things grow, transplanting, rearranging, moving a plant from here to there or setting out young seedlings. We all share the same keen pleasure and satisfaction in watching young plants adjust to a new area. How many times a day do Bob and I go out and take a look at our tomatoes? Perhaps we water, or maybe we just touch, and admire the new plants and guess how soon we'll be eating the lettuces.

The "farm" as we labeled this minigarden is just beyond the strawberries. To our delight the strawberries are growing redder day by day. They are sort of tear-drop shaped, an upside-down tear. Catherine the Great is lending an aristocratic note to our place!

A few minutes ago Bob brought in the first ripe strawberry. We halved it and each had one morsel of goodness. And now, with figs coming, we're really going to have produce! Lurking deep in my mind is the idea of a persimmon tree. They *do* grow here. I wonder if we should have one. Friends shared some of their fruit with us last year and it was marvelous. Imagine being able to pick not only figs but persimmons.

I thought we had reached the peak of amusement and incredibility with last fall's catalogues. But I see I was wrong. Today the mail brings a new one and idly glancing through the pages I am startled to come upon something called a "to-pato."

"You've *got* to be wrong," said Bob, when I told him about it. "That is absolutely impossible."

Together we pored over the page to read that the topato combines two plants into one space to produce a bumper crop of both plump juicy tomatoes above ground and large luscious potatoes beneath the soil!

This catalogue comes from California and, judging from past experience, amazing and marvelous things happen in that state. Here is evidence!

A fine friendship has developed between me and some dogwood blossoms in a vase by my bed.

I seem to be in the middle of having the flu, and Bob brought these beautiful blossoms to me from out in the garden where they are gloriously in full flower.

How can I have the flu when "Spring Is Bustin' Out All Over"? How can I be sick when all outdoors is burgeoning with life, health and vitality?

I lie here and commune with the dogwood. It's pink dogwood, a special tone of pink. The petals vary in color, deeper in parts, lighter in parts. They are lighter near the center and the outer edges. What particularly enchants me is the soft and live texture of the petals. A beautiful rhythm of swirls enhances each one, swirls that catch the eye and lead it around like in a dance. What I am calling "petals" are really bracts. In the center of the four bracts are tiny green-white buds in a tight cluster that open a few at a time. Each of these miniscule florets has four petals and four tiny shinygold stamens standing upright.

Having the flu is a humbling experience, as is any sickness. Moving along through normal living we make plans and follow through on them; we make decisions and carry them out. We live with a sense of having our days pretty well in line.

But when you get sick the helm of the ship has flown right out of your hands. You have unwittingly relinquished your authority over yourself and your life to entirely unpredictable forces. Things well beyond you take over and you feel as if the proverbial rug had been pulled right out from under you. The humbling part of being sick is when you realize that these things can happen to any one of us at any time. We can be thrown out of health, temporarily robbed of a sense of well-being, and pushed through a few knot-holes of physical discomfort.

Now and then I'd get up and walk about in the living room, or sit in the sun in the window and look at the garden. With binoculars I brought each new flower into my lap and every bee seeking nectar became an enormous Land of Oz creature.

How can you feel so fine one day and so awful the next and for days thereafter? I used to ask myself.

Fortunately, I soon stopped protesting and let go of all speculation and wondering. I was where I was and I'd better just accept. When sickness happens, there isn't a thing to do but accept where you are and go along with procedures for getting better. And to think positively, if possible, which it isn't always. It's worth trying though because it has been said, and I believe it, that when we are freed from negative thinking the body has the power to do its own healing.

So one day I awoke feeling different.

89

Some little shred of me was back. The moment of turning had arrived. Some basic strength within me was asserting itself. Things were different. I could smell and taste and had coughed less during the night. I combed my hair and put on lipstick. All at once I cared. When you're getting better, be it only an inch at a time, your spirits soar. My first day out I sat in the sunshine in a chair, wrapped in a blanket, and in a state of utter bliss as I smelled all the spring scents and took in the colors everywhere. There was a cardinal singing and today his tune was "better, better, better."

A little green lizard emerged from somewhere and darted along the top of the picket fence, blowing his throat out into a succession of small orange bubbles. This the lizards do when courting, but where was his mate? Watching that companionable little creature really confirmed my recovery.

Across the terrace a small brown lizard, the first one's relative no doubt, was sleeping on the bricks in the sun. I love these little animals. They take me back to when I used to haunt the pet shops in New

York City after school and save my allowance for buying chameleons, turtles and goldfish. But to see them here in their natural state, sometimes dozing, relaxed and brown, or green and excited and blowing out orange bubbles, is the greatest of pleasures.

While I was appreciating the lizards Bob was watering all the little new plants—some white petunias and some deep purple ones, and some miniature marigolds. Neighbors from across the street came over, bringing Florida oranges and grapefruit. We all sat in the sun and talked a while. I thoroughly enjoyed being a part of life again.

Later, inside the house, I made a custard. I went back to bed after these exertions, but at least I had made it, accomplished some *one* thing, and I was participating in the active world again. How I savored lying on the terrace every morning, feeling my strength return day by day. *Gracias a Dios*, as the Spanish say for each good thing.

Most of the time I forget about age, but having just recovered from the flu it comes to mind. My mother, a vigorous person with a perpetual sense of fun and readiness to laugh, once said at the age of ninety-two, "You know, you never feel old inside. It's just your outsides and when you look in the mirror." This reminds me of May Sarton, who wrote of growing older: "The mirror tells only the facts, never the poetry." The body doesn't always do what you want it to do as you get older, but I agree with my mother. Your spirit need never feel old!

It was clear and cold the day of the steeplechase. Betty and her husband, Norme, and Bob and I set forth with blankets, mats, chairs and a picnic lunch. There's no more beautiful spot than Tryon for this annual event. Rolling meadows, backed by woods with dogwood in full flower, redbud, and the new spring green on all the trees. Everyone was laughing and gay and friendly as we selected a sunny location on the hillside. It was good to be right above the paddock, where they walk the horses around before each race. The course encircles the crowd, with a number of jumps here and there. From our hillside we could see the finish line. Of course you meet all your friends, most of whom are picnicking too.

As much fun as anything was watching the horses that were about to race being led around and around. We know nothing about horses but we had a pool of ten cents each. If no one won, the pool accumulated. It was so amusing, with our utter lack of knowledge, to study the horses as they circled. Was this one too skittish? No, he'd not the endurance nor the discipline to win. That lovely chestnut, whose coat shone in the sun, looked a little more stable, but did he have quite the drive? And there was one with a wild look in his eye. No one could put a saddle on him at all! Finally, all the horses were saddled and numbered and the race would start. We were entertained by the names of the different entries—half the time we chose winners by name. Who could resist "Streak-Lightning" or "Moonshine" or "Comet" or "High Tor"?

We watched several races from up on the hillside, then walked down through the greenest grass across the brook. For one race we stood right up against the railing. The horses would go twice around the course. They passed a mere few feet away.

The gathered force and energy in each animal as he skimmed by so close made my spine tingle. There was skill and beauty in the way the jockey balanced too, never sitting, but crouching. He and the horse were one as they flew by. I had the strangest sensation as we watched them pass the second time; I seemed to have absorbed some of their gathered, directed force and power. I have stood at the edge of the ocean after a storm and watched breakers pound on the sand. There by the sea some of the strength of the waves seeped into me. I've watched a thunderstorm in summer and felt the wind's force stir and waken some inner sense of courage and strength. And now, on this sunny afternoon, looking at a horse race, I had the same exciting sense of response to the force and vigor of galloping horses.

Later we walked up close to a jump and watched these beautiful animals soar over. Surely they were not of this earth. Horse and rider floated through the air, so lightly and gracefully did they cross the bars. Man and mount seemed one, so sensitive was the jockey to every mood and movement of the creature under him.

At first it was amusing to find out who won and add up our dimes and then, all of a sudden, watching and feeling the motion became more important than winning; in fact it became everything. The whole afternoon was exhilarating and the four of us came home in a fine mood to relive it all again.

Cellars of houses are to me particularly interesting, especially with hot-air furnaces. The numerous air ducts around the ceiling are like the branches of a large, ancient and gnarled tree. I sometimes think of them as great arms, lifting, undergirding, and supporting the floor above and the people who live there. They certainly seem like welcome and vital undergirdings when a winter wind blows.

A few days ago our son Bob and my husband, Bob, and I were all standing down in the cellar contemplating the possibility of turning a part of it into a guest bedroom, bath, and kitchenette with an outside deck. Son Bob, an architect in San Francisco, did the design for the remodelling job here in Tryon before we moved in. Now here he was making another plan for us. He spent part of his visit here at my desk before reams of drafting paper with frequent trips to the cellar.

"If we're going to have our guests stay down in the cellar," Bob senior said, "we can't call it a cellar any more. We'll have to dignify it with some other name."

Basement? Just as bad.

First floor? But it isn't. Lower deck? perhaps. We'll have to ponder this one.

We didn't let our son work all the time though. One idyllic sunny morning we took off with a picnic lunch and the top down for Green River Cove, where we drove all through the area, picnicking on a little beach beside the river where there were rapids and white froth tossing and swirling around the rocks. Spring had spilled its generous abundance all through the cove.

Yesterday we experienced one of those satisfying responses of nature. There was a honeysuckle sprawling out where its beauty was not appreciated because it was half hidden in grass. The coral-pink firecrackerlike blossoms were scarcely visible.

"How lovely that would look spilling over the woodpile at one end of the garden," I suggested.

Bob, who considers woodpiles and everything pertaining to firewood more or less sacred, took a dim view of this, so we settled for planting it against the fence where part would go up the pickets if we tied it, and the rest would tumble discreetly over one end of the woodpile. Bob would permit this, and I had to admit that this was a better place, in fact ideal.

It had been misting and moisty for a couple of days when Bob moved the honeysuckle. We began by lifting up the runners. Some went along the ground surface ten feet, sending down roots along the way. We would have a number of plants to give away. Gladys had said she would love one, and Banks too. We separated new plants, gathered up the main stalk and lifted it out. Because the ground was wet it was easy to move and the earth was soft and diggable. Late yesterday afternoon we did this transplanting, tying up long branches onto the fence, letting a little spill over the woodpile. The line of pickets that had seemed rather stark and bare was greatly enhanced by the graceful curving greenery. In fact, we were pleased by the whole effect.

What a satisfaction to waken in the night and hear a real hard rain! This was nature's response. Bob's hunch to move the honeysuckle yesterday was a good one. This morning the whole plant looked marvelous, no droop. It won't know it was moved. The rain is also aiding our other transplants—the petunias, marigolds, the ajuga recently set outside the fence along the road, and the new primroses.

Wayside Gardens has the custom of packing things in a kind of plastic nubbles that exactly resemble peanuts. So entertaining are these! The little primrose plants that came earlier this month seemed tiny and ineffective until we got them out of the pots; then we were enormously impressed by the size and strength of the roots. This is how it is with Wayside material.

Looking outside this morning we could see a faint rim of pale yellow powder at the edge of the puddles on the brick terrace —the first pine pollen! Next month this forerunner will remind us that the seasons are never static. We are always moving on from one month to the next, and from one season to another.

Our ajuga is a blue carpet, and from one angle it leads up to the foot of one of the prettiest snowy-white azaleas I have ever seen. The bush is like a festival, a wedding. All outdoors, rain or shine, it is a miracle of wonder.

By the door a lovely lavender azalea with huge blooms is full out. The flowers are drooping in the rain, each blossom a ballet dancer with an orchid-colored skirt, long and full. One tiny fire pink is out, scarlet and brilliant. And the first rhododendron, a cluster of pinkish-red frilled with stamens, with the flower parts curving and graceful. The new andromeda leaves, shiny rusty red and pale green, are as appealing as any flower can be.

Where there was a stretch of dead leaves for weeks there are now countless little slender stems of maidenhair fern. The uncurling fronds are like buttonhooks or pin curls of smoky pink. Each hour they open a little more.

Back in the winter I wrote letters to the

family, to erstwhile neighbors in Connecticut, and to old friends everywhere. Why? To ask them if they would write a letter to Bob but send it discreetly to me for the occasion of his very special birthday this year. Would the children say what it meant to them to have him for a father? The neighbors for a neighbor? Our friends for a friend?

Letters began coming and I stashed them away. Of course Bob was suspicious because I wouldn't let him see certain letters and quickly tucked them out of sight. But he was good natured about it!

Fran and Mark, who are among our oldest friends, also have birthdays the same week in April, and Mark retired last month. So this makes a great number of reasons for the four of us celebrating together. They joined us down here for a gala few days of spring and outdoors and all the sharings of old friends. Then came the great evening. There was the rustle of tissue paper in the house all day. Dinner was early, and ended with a fabulous chocolate angel cake with three candles, one for the past, one for the present, and one for the future. Afterward there were presents, and I always receive some nonbirthday presents to console me. The climax was the pile of letters, tied with ribbon that was presented to Bob. He read them all aloud and we all were moved by the expressions of warmth and nostalgic remembering coming to him from all directions.

Of course they made Bob feel magnificent. Every one was as different as were the people who wrote them. Many of the letters, especially from the family, slipped back through the years, recalling incidents involving Bob that were meaningful to the writer. Some days later Bob told me that reading these letters from friends and family everywhere had given him a particular kind of confidence and a lasting sense of well-being, of being loved for what he was. And further than this they made him realize that here is something we all can do for our friends, in fact for all people everywhere. Tell them the things we especially appreciate about them, as they occur to us, or as we recall them, whenever an occasion presents itself. Why not do this more often?

What a moving and stirring evening the

four of us had, participating in these meaningful birthdays. Before going to bed Bob and I stepped out onto the terrace to look at the stars. Tonight they no longer tangle in bare branches but are hidden, some of them, behind leaves. But some we could see.

The foliage tells us that summer is really near. As we looked out, the water in our tiny pool was black. No, now a few stars shimmered across it, and one star, caught just there, grew brighter as the water stilled.

5

May Is a Green World

"DO look, it's as large as a dinner plate!"

"Come now, Jean. Don't exaggerate! A dessert plate maybe," said our neighbor Homer.

We were gazing in wonder at the clematis on the outside of our fence. Lanuginosa is its botanical name and I never saw anything so immense. When fully open the great white petals surround a feathery center, and the blossoms hang in clusters, overlapping each other against the fence. On another part of the fence is blue clematis, with equally enormous flowers. This one is more an African violet shade than blue, a very deep tone. The blossoms of both the blue and the white clematis make attractive indoor arrangements, lasting for many days. I float them in a low silver bowl given us years back for a wedding present.

The surprising part of the blue-violet clematis is that the plant itself seems to be so filled with enthusiasm for this deep color that it sends some of it into the leaves as well as the flowers—as if it had an overabundance of pigment and couldn't let it go to waste! Some of the green foliage up near the blossoms is casually but definitely streaked with light lavender. While Homer, and Bob who had joined us, were admiring the clematis I went in to get a ruler. The biggest bloom measured eight inches from petal tip to petal tip. Dessert plate? Dinner plate?

May in Tryon is a green world. The leaves are fully out now and growing larger every day. Wherever we look, we are surrounded by green. And on a rainy day the color deepens and strengthens. Look out the window anywhere into our woods and your eye is carried on and on into greenery, and your spirit too is bathed in greenness.

Those who study colors and their effects say green promotes serenity. Is it any wonder that when we walk down the path to the brook through this world of green we return in a dreamy, relaxed state? I have always found green a soothing color, a gentle tone, and I love wearing it. Now we both appreciate our spring immersion in it. We eat on the porch these days, and look into treetops at each meal. Today for lunch we had the company of a small gray squirrel stretched along a branch just outside the screening. His fluffy tail floated up and folded along his back to his head. He was lying still as could be, watching us with a bright and beady black eye.

And all the while, the sun filtering through the leaves was giving us many different tints—a golden green where rays dusted the foliage, bluer shades in the pine shadows. Every tone of this favorite color permeates the woods reaching beneath the trees. Backgrounding the greens and blending them together is the rich earth, reddish-orange in places, and a warm toasty brown where pine needles and dead leaves cover.

The successive waves of dazzling spring garden flowers have now passed but all is not over. Out near the clematis our Blaze rose is unfolding the brightest of red flowers, and at the fringes of the garden, and up the mountain road beyond us, wild flowers are opening everywhere.

Bob has just laid the annual fresh pine bark on the garden path. We have been digging out the ajuga and wild iris that would grow right over this path if we'd permit. We've shared at least two bushels with friends. I took several clusters of iris down to the brook, to the new terrace there. We planted these beside the stream and splashed water over them. The new table and benches made from the ancient and massive oak beams of an old log cabin look magnificent. One day we'll bring a picnic down and eat here among the wild yellow and flame azaleas. It is cool along the stream and soon the weather will be warm enough to make the shade and the running water an invitation not to resist.

Our garden path is particularly appealing this month. There is the jack-in-the-pulpit nearly a yard high. What graceful swirls and circles pattern the pulpit. The wild low-growing iris has almost as much charm now as when in flower. Lush wide leaves folding over in clusters provide an interesting texture. The Burford holly nearby has grown fabulously this spring, and is loaded with green berries. We'll have to have a festival in its honor next fall when the berries redden.

Yesterday Bob and I spread plant food on the azaleas to assure good summer growth and ample flowering next year. I swoop back the mulch and Bob scatters a trowelful, or two, for each bush. As we replace the mulch we feel extremely benificent, as you do when you feed plants. It's a deep and satisfying pleasure to garden together on a glorious sunny day with the air mild and caressing, the gentlest of breezes, and a pair of summer tanagers playing in the magnolia. These two beauties were enjoying the last of the suet in the wire feeder attached to the trunk of the oak. I hadn't realized how yellow the female was, a deep shade of old gold. No scarlet can be more brilliant than the tint of the feathers on the head of the male.

One of our excitements these days is the Southern magnolia tree: the buds we were trying to locate with the binoculars last month seem to have sprung into being and multiplied. Each day we discover more. We had at first thought there would be only two or three or maybe four because it was the tree's first year to flower. But no, we are counting the eighteenth, the nineteenth, and the twentieth. From the top to the base of the tree, and nestled in among shiny green leaves, perky upright buds stand, growing larger and fatter daily and turning slowly from green to white. Alas, I fear we shall miss them, though, because at the end of the month we're driving north. They have a lot of growing to do before they will open into those great dramatic white blossoms that are so exotic and fragrant. Oh well, there's always another year.

We were moving about in the garden, Bob and I, peacefully doing a little of this and that, when a dear friend and her husband arrived with a batch of delectable cupcakes still warm from the oven. What a cook she is!

We wandered all about the garden eating cupcakes, nibbling bright red strawberries, and admiring everything, including the tomatoes and the sage. The young lettuces planted a few weeks ago were cheery and crisp and one inch high, and a vivid green against the rich red earth. They had grown considerably in last night's rain.

There are few activities that engage us more thoroughly and absorbingly these days than gardening. And gardening is an occupation of particular nowness. In weeding this, planting that, pruning the other, we are thoroughly meshed with what we are doing. No alien thought intrudes. This is how it usually is when you work with growing things you love. While absorbed in the current experience, through it we touch a kind of infinity. We are in a nowness utterly free from the tangle of yesterday's regrets and equally free from tomorrow's apprehensions and anxieties.

People, I think, are a lot more than their beliefs and opinions, more than their ideas and habits. There is something in each of us that reaches farther than we consciously know. The most stirring moments come as we become aware of and touch this "more" in another person or in ourselves. This mysterious "more" has in it, surely, some of the elements of where the individual is going, where he is headed, as well as where he has been. It is perhaps the fleeting spark of divinity that lives in every one of us that is much greater, deeper, vaster than the opinions we hold, than the beliefs that sometimes concern us.

The profusion of Oregon "grapes" hanging in great clusters and trailing over spiney leaves are turning a soft and dusty blue against their red stems. And bluer every day. A cat bird tailored gray, sleek and smooth, sings from the top of the picket fence and then darts down to flutter among the berries for his breakfast. He takes one in his bill and holds it a minute. Savoring the treat ahead? One quick movement and it is gone. He swallows the blue berry whole and then hops about among the branches for another.

A little bright green inchworm is measuring the page of my book as I sit reading on the terrace. To me there is something especially appealing about this small creature. I watch him move along. Every now and then he reaches his front end up into the air, stretching around curiously, lest he miss something.

These days our walks have added glamour. Everywhere locust trees are in full flower, trailing white blossoms down through the foliage and spreading their sweet fragrance far and wide. Toward noon and at dusk the scent seems unusually strong as we walk up the mountain road beyond our place. Bordering the roads everywhere, the honeysuckle is beginning to open and the delicious aromas of the two mingle.

When we drive about with the top down we are bathed in both these scents and many others that we don't identify and that can change every hundred feet or so. This is the month not only of greenery but of fragrances.

Along the roadsides graceful arching branches of flowering blackberries tangle through scrubby open places. Tall blue and gold iris fill gardens, while little chipmunks with perky tails dart across the road ahead of the car to disappear in the leaves.

All month we have watched the deep green that is May creep slowly up the mountains toward the summits. It started in the warm valleys, this color, and gradually worked toward the peaks. Earlier in the month the mountain tops were bare-branched and gray. At first a light yellow-green appeared dusting the upper shoulders. Little by little this changed to a deeper tone and now all the ranges are a deep rich green from top to bottom.

At Gladys and Carl's a cardinal is nesting in a bush outside the front door. Nothing is quieter or stiller than a mother bird sitting on eggs. Three eggs, they say. Betty tells us Norme is hunting grubs and worms every day through the woods. "Is he going fishing?" I asked. No, a pileated woodpecker came to their feeder and seems unable to fly. But nothing broken: they believe it must be old age. Norme's current project is to see that the bird is fed, and it has an enormous appetite.

Every now and then there is a day when we have a shower almost every hour. On such days the greenness seems almost to float off the foliage and fill the very air. The rains flow over the red brick terrace in rivers. Some of the showers come so fast and heavily that the down pipes from the gutters can't manage, and water spurts from all the seams, creating enchanting little waterfalls in various places along the roof.

This is spring in Tryon that began weeks ago, that goes on and on with lovely fresh new things happening each day in mountains, in woods, in gardens, and in the hearts of us all.

One of the best ways to experience this wonderful thing called spring fever is to merge with it. Relax and follow your impulses—maybe wander down and eat a sandwich by the stream, possibly sit on an old log and do nothing but feel and be one with your surroundings. Yield to any and all urges and enjoy! Our love for exploring back roads in the deep country is one way of giving in to this annual state that submerges us like a wave.

Yesterday we started out in the late afternoon with a map of Polk County. Having the top down as we drive along is a special pleasure and helps us to feel part of the fields and the mountains that rise up in the distance. We're never exactly sure where we are, nor do we care. It's pleasant to slightly lose ourselves.

And so we roam. How green is this field of timothy and how black the cattle grazing in it. Along the dirt road comes a little girl riding a pony bareback. She is barefoot and her long blond hair shines in the sun. We pass a field surrounded by a split rail fence, which zigzags through golden drifts of St. John's wort, and just beyond flourishes a stretch of blue chicory—blue as the sky above. I stop to pick armfuls of both. They will wilt a little before we get home but a soak in cold water will revive them. From somewhere come sounds of chickens and a rooster crowing. How welcome this is. I can just eat so many eggs before I need to hear the sound of a live and wandering chicken. And the same with vegetables. Every so often I like to see them growing —I almost need to. The earth is our source. Watching the things we use, live with, eat and wear grow in it is one way of opening ourselves to an appreciation of forces and depths beyond us. Isn't this another way we feel the touch of the earth?

Now we have come to a field of red soil with neat rows of produce, onions and beans and lettuce, and beyond rows of cabbage. How beautiful the cabbage is against the brilliant orange-red earth of North Carolina.

We hear the song of a meadowlark. One is perching on a light wire above. I can see the black "V" on its breast. From somewhere three more meadowlarks appear and fly over another bright green field where black crows are floating. And along the side of the road wave beautiful grasses with red feathery tops. Occasional whiffs of onion grass drift our way.

We keep passing small homes. Some are trailers where people live, some farms, and here is a silo, a great gray barn and a herd of brown cows. Among the cows are a few horses; a white one glows in the sunlight. At a crossroad we pause.

Three beautiful dirt roads lie before us. Which shall we take? In the "V" between two stands an old log cabin with a chimney made of fieldstones and the chinks between the aged logs are stuffed with red earth. I mark a cross on the map. I will come back and paint this someday. The open door hangs crookedly. And ghosts of the past rise up in the dooryard. I can envision the black cauldron over the outdoor fire as the mistress of the house does her washing. And this reminds me of the instructions of a mountain woman to her daughter on how to wash clothes. This we saw in the restored Cade's Cove area when we were camping over that way. After specific directions on sorting the clothes and so forth, the advice continued: "Throw the rinse water on the flowers, clean the privy with the soap water. Put on a clean dress, comb your hair, brew a cup of tea, set and rest a while and count your blessings."

A little beyond the log cabin we saw a marvelous, aged two-story frame house. The roof was gabled. The house was very upright with a roofed front porch. The open door was an invitation. We got out and prowled around. While wandering through deserted rooms and stepping over holes in the floor, we slipped back years and began to imagine the rooms peopled with a family. I could almost feel the warmth of a fire in the blackened fireplace, and smell a great stew simmering. Houses have their own particular vibrations, built into the very walls by the life that has been lived in them. And years later a visitor may catch some of these.

After driving another couple of hours, Bob took map in hand to figure out where we were and to head back. A wonderful spring afternoon—a wonderful spring impulse.

Sometimes I have troubles with the world!

The dreadful events that occur in far places tend to move in on me, upset me enormously, and take over my emotions.

I cannot view these aggressions and international troubles, as many people do, as history in the making, and fascinating to follow. Neither can I consider them as political maneuvers. I can only see them as people hurting. As men intentionally causing other men to hurt physically, mentally and emotionally. This distresses me beyond description. I see us living in a world where there is a need to build, not destroy; to love, not hate; where everyone of us needs to be loved, appreciated, cared for, and needs to love, appreciate and care for others.

Anaïs Nin writes "It is not my destiny to live the drama of death, war, agony, hunger. It is my destiny to live the drama of feeling and imagination, reality and unreality, a drama underlying the other, a drama without guns, dynamite, without explosions."

I find as I grow older, when I become immersed in a difficult or unpleasant experience, that unless I can act and fight the cruelty I am hearing about or witnessing, I have to inwardly leave the situation and turn to another world.

Some people in observing the suffering that occurs far across the world identify with it. Occasionally this distant vision causes them not to be aware of the fears and frustrations of those nearby. For some strange reason, I cannot seem to see the agonies on the other side of the globe to the same extent that I am aware of what is going on immediately around me. I am more conscious of what is happening to the person who lives down the street, who works in the market, or the gift shop, or the post office; or my next-door neighbor. And of course we all have friends who tell us of their own challenges and problems. I seldom listen to the radio or follow the news in the papers, and for this reason I come in for some criticism by people who feel I'm an escapist. Am I? I wonder.

I'm certainly not unaware, indifferent, or blind. But actually I see no sense or reason in experiencing or expressing futile rage and discouragement with world affairs, politics, man's inhumanity to man, and his cruelty. I have no desire to add to the despair of the world my own personal sufferings over what goes on a long distance off. If I had any idea of what I could do to help, I would do it. Apart from writing letters to the President and to the senators occasionally, I can think of no other act of mine that would change and improve any of the dreadful things that are happening in countries far, far off.

I think I realize and have accepted the fact that my present role is to create or try to create where I live an atmosphere in which people can breathe and rebuild their courage, confidence, and sense of joy.

I'm proud of the many wonderful organizations in this country which help alleviate sorrow and suffering in far off places. I'm proud of the people who work in these causes. They unselfishly follow their urges as I follow mine and I admire them enormously. We contribute as we can to a goodly number of such organizations. But I have become sharply aware of the fact that sometimes the people we see and know who have a roof over their heads, plenty to eat, and all physical needs met, are often in great need of help. I'm speaking of a different kind of help. These people often need a friend's understanding, warmth, love. Just someone to listen to them. In groups I have from time to time sensed an individual's distress and unmet need. Perhaps my deepest concern is to try to help here. This seems more pertinent to me right now than what goes on on the other side of the world.

All the dye kettles are out in a shiny, glowing white array on the kitchen counter this rainy morning. A good time to dye more wool before putting rug and equipment away for the summer. I feel like some kind of witch standing over the stove, stirring the great "cauldron" filled with dark liquid. With the tongs I dip in wet white woolen strips, dunking them up and down and stirring them about. It is exciting to watch them absorb the color, and see the dye disappear right into the wool while the water grows lighter and lighter. Incredibly, it soon becomes quite clear.

A little time in the oven for all the gay colors to set. And now the bathroom is enhanced with countless brilliant strips of vivid tones that defy this rainy day's grayness. Actually these rainy spring days are as lovely as the clear ones—the tree trunks are dark and wet and beautiful, emphasizing as they do all the verticals in the woods. Spring rain has such a growing quality to it I can almost feel the earthiness and growth when I walk out in the garden. This I have to do quite frequently, rain or no rain. Some people don't like rain but rain to a gardener is nature's blessing.

Besides the shine of the forest, the woods shine I mentioned before, there is a shine of vitality in the plants. Before breakfast I stepped out into the garden and stopped by an andromeda bush. This particular one has concerned us. Thus far this season it has no new growth or leaves like its neighbors. Is it going to die? The leaves are dull, no single bud of new foliage is visible anywhere. We have been watching this plant for some weeks. The one next to it has a feel of vigor, of life and a crispness and shine on its abundant new leaves—a shine of life. Now, studying the ailing plant, I saw down among the twigs some almost hidden fresh, beginning leaves unfolding. New leaves after all! Surely now it would revive. We could let go of our concern.

In healthy plants there is a vital quality revealed in firm foliage, and a kind of shine. This you can see and, even more, you can feel.

In healthy, fulfilled people there is also a shine, a kind of sparkle, a glow that emanates from them. This you become immediately conscious of when you are with them. You can warm yourself by this quality in another.

The magic of May is not outward beauty alone but something intangible, indescribable. It is something you feel, something you hear with an inner ear, something you sense deep within.

But this thing called spring, the special enchantment that is May, is a thing you cannot grasp and hold. It's not static for one instant but possesses the everchanging quality that tells you things are happening and constantly emerging. You feel this when you look about you at the subtleties of growth, the altering shapes, the changing light and warming weather. It is all of these and more blended together that compose this appealing month.

May is stretching ahead toward summer,

toward fall and even winter and the following May. You cannot hold back life that is ever reaching forward toward fulfillment. But you can merge and move with it, and feel yourself an element in it all. At this season we say with the Buddhist "The self is more than his own being. It includes the whole Universe."

Perhaps the lesson of May is that we can move with the leisurely grace that comes with the natural progress of things from one state to the next. This is quiet and gradual change, motion with serenity, sure and continuous and never hurried. This is the time of year when we learn to receive, to love, and to let go. Always ready to loose and let go. As long as we remember to loose and let go we have it—the message, the essence, the excitement and wonder of this season. This is paradox but a fact.

We were just finishing breakfast when the phone rang.

"Tracy and I are going down to pick strawberries," said Banks. "You are probably too busy packing to come but—"

"Not necessarily," I interrupted.

Ever since we moved South we had heard

of the great fields of strawberries in Campobello, where you can gather all you want. I'd been yearning to go. One of my happiest memories is of picking strawberries as a child. We children would go out to the berry patch in my father's garden, taking with us a bowl of sugar and another small bowl of heavy cream, skimmed in great creases from one of the large flat milk pans in the pantry. We'd sit in the sunlight picking the berries, dunking them first in cream and then in sugar. What a heavenly experience! If you have done this as a child, you also have something very special to remember!

In two seconds on the phone all this had flashed through my mind.

"You know, we just might be able to come," I said. "Tell me how to get there."

We had things pretty well in hand and were leaving for the North day after tomorrow. It's the week ahead of time that I become bogged down and slightly frenzied. Usually the last day or two I'm rather calm and everything is organized.

Bob, however, was just settling down to write a letter, a business letter and rather important to get off before our departure. He had a sort of faraway look in his eyes, sitting there before the typewriter. And I came busting in with my idea of going to pick strawberries.

I guess he knew how much I wanted to go, because his yielding was beautiful and gracious. It was clear and sunny and early enough not to be too hot. We had never before been in that particular rolling farmland with the great fields of wild flowers—countless daisies, white and yellow, vetch all covered with purple flowers, banks of wild morning glories and countless other unfamiliar varieties. We are more used to the woodland flowers, but here we were in the midst of meadow flowers and I think I'd never seen so many.

Now we were on a stretch of high land with the Tryon ranges in the distance and in the foreground the road, bordered with red earth, wound through wild flower meadows. Here and there was a checkerboard of red fields, newly ploughed, alternating with green ones already planted and growing.

We curved around, now left, now right, following signs, red paint on boards spelling "strawberries" with an arrow pointing. The enormous field was dotted through with a dozen or so people, all picking. We soon discovered Banks and Tracy and joined them and our baskets began to fill. Such flourishing plants, and between the rows there was hay, clean and comfortable to kneel on. Here a glint of red and there another revealed berries among the large healthy saw-edged leaves. It was a pleasure to sit in one place, feeling the sun warm on my back and exploring for the ripest berries. They were all beautiful, the bright red ones, the part red ones, those still pure ivory that hung in clusters were equally enchanting. I never saw so many berries in all my life! And such an easy camaraderie among the pickers. The woman on one side of me was taking hers home to make strawberry preserve to use on ice cream. Her husband's favorite dessert. Pretty often we had to eat an especially ripe one! A just-picked strawberry, warm from the sun, has a flavor impossible to describe. We ate and picked and crawled along on the clean, bouncy hay. The four of us were talking and laughing and oh-ing and ah-ing when suddenly anyone of us would discover a plant with an especially good crop of berries. Since we were leaving so soon we were not prepared to freeze or make jam as the others were, but we decided that we were going to have one fabulous farewell shortcake—our last dinner tomorrow! With real cream! Might as well go overboard!

When Bob and I each had a quart we gave one to Banks and Tracy and took the other with us. We left our friends there among the strawberry rows while we drove home to a house scattered all over with piles of things to take up north. Next morning I was beating up shortcake while Bob began to pack the car. By noon the car was full and we were really ready for departure. We had our last dinner with dessert of strawberry shortcake, the whipped cream spreading over the berries like drifts of snow.

When I first wakened, the sky, low toward the horizon, was a warm ivory. The mountains are completely lost to view now but a golden tint in the air assures us of sunshine. I was up early, excitedly aware of the promise ahead. One of my southern friends calls it being "journey proud," when she gets so stirred up and exhilarated that she cannot sleep too well before taking off on a holiday. So it was with me this last night at home.

After breakfast, when the sun was shining down and the day's promise fulfilled, a cardinal sang us a farewell from the top of the liquid amber tree while a towhee added his music to the air. I wandered out to take a last look at the garden—the maidenhair fern, the flourishing bed of new annuals, and the cucumber—I'm sure it's going to stay now. The tomatoes are thriving, and I listen for the sound of the brook and breathe deeply of the fragrance of the woods, green and growing. It's a perfect day. A kind of inner excitement fills me.

The car is full. Did I remember? Did you remember? We are off.

6

June By The Sea

WHEN we drew up in front of our house on Cape Cod I wondered if I'd be able to get out. We had paused in the village for groceries, and for six bright red geraniums in full flower for each side of the front entrance. With all these interesting things and mail besides we were both pretty well packed in. It was almost enough to sit there in the car and look at our beloved Flutery.

The Flutery stands, with other summer cottages, on land virtually surrounded by water. Along the broad white sandy beach on one side break the waves of the Atlantic Ocean. This we call the big, or outer, beach. On the other side from where we are lies the inlet, and Mill Pond. Between the outer beach and Mill Pond is a channel where the tide rushes in and out, and rests quietly at full high or low. Bordering this channel on the far side, great marshes reach inland for miles, marshes that turn pure gold in October and where the heron and other interesting shore birds feed at all seasons.

Here is the Flutery before us now with its backdrop of deep-blue Mill Pond, blue channel and marshes. It is trim and small and gray shingled with a red brick chimney and a bright yellow door.

I'll explain the Flutery. Years back, when our three children were small, we used to spend our summers in East Orleans. We built a house with a bowed roof, a picket fence, a front garden, a number of bedrooms and bunks and a wonderful old wood stove in the kitchen. It stood out on the bluff with a superb view over the ocean—and there was nothing between us and Spain! We could see the sun and the moon rise up out of the sea and watch ocean liners and fishing fleets sail along the horizon. We also built a little guest house we called the Flutery, because we used to gather there to play bamboo flutes that we made ourselves. Tucked away in the little guest house we were free from the rest of the household, and could be as off key as we usually were, and no one the less happy!

When the children grew up and got married we sold the big house and moved the little guest house across the bluff to a piece of land along the inlet. We built onto it a bunk room, another bedroom, a kitchenette, and installed a floor furnace. It became the perfect tiny house and completely comfortable for two people. We rent it summers but enjoy it ourselves in spring or fall, and in all weather the furnace and the Franklin stove keep it warm and cozy.

Our spring arrival is invariably fraught with suspense lest we miss the lilacs, but this year we caught them full out. We gradually unwound ourselves from the recent purchases and emerged from the car to be almost overcome by the fragrance and beauty of these blossoms. Large dark purple clusters of flowers bent down over the car when Bob stopped it by the entrance. Tossing feathery blooms in lighter shades nearly hid the greenery by the yellow front door. Off to the left were white lilacs, masses of snowy foam turning the bush into a large bouquet. Tipping over the roof from the far side of the house were both whites and lavenders.

These lilacs have an interesting history. Some years back I felt that a great clump of lilacs in a deserted locust grove next to the church really should have suckers taken away from their bases to be better bushes! Bob, being Bob, would have none of this, so one night, by the light of a full moon, a friend and I set forth to dig up some of the seedling bushes. Dark and wavering junipers and the nearby lichen-covered gravestones made of the whole project an eerie adventure. Every one we dug up was a mere single whip with a wavering root or two. Being gardeners, both of us, we were scrupulously careful not to disturb the main shrubs. We each got half a dozen or so bushes to plant around our houses. This must have been more than twenty years ago and now the plants are higher than the roof and six to eight feet across. I must touch these flowers, run my hands over the great masses of florets in each cluster, sometimes as many as seven separate flower heads in one spray.

There is a delicate softness in these blooms as you feel them, and at the same time a vitality and freshness. There must be a million florets on each bush. But lilacs should not be counted. They should be smelled, touched, loved and lived with.

As soon as the groceries were put away and the suitcases stowed, I picked some lilacs for the bedroom, the living room, the kitchen, dining table and bathroom. And that first night we not only ate supper surrounded by their aroma but drifted off to sleep to the sweet fragrance.

But before supper even we wander down on the beach. We have to go to the shore almost immediately when we first reach Nauset. It was late afternoon, the tide was high. Terns were drifting on the inlet, and flying over the water. Now and then one would dive for a small fish, and come up with it glinting in its bill.

What caught our eyes at once were pieces of driftwood—driftwood washed up in the beach grass in a variety of sizes and shapes. It was chilly, and we would pick up enough in a few minutes to have a fire in the Franklin stove that first night. Driftwood is a lovely shade of silvery gray and streaked with rust where old nails used to be and sometimes still are. The more old nails and rusty stains the prettier the colors will be in our fire.

Here by the sea Bob's rapport and affection for firewood settles on driftwood. Every time we went to the beach those first days we brought back a little. A pile is gradually accumulating behind the house. Often I hear Bob out there with the axe chopping lengths to fit the Franklin stove. There's something different and special about the aroma of burning driftwood. Perhaps it has soaked up elements and minerals from the sea and now gives them back to us in the darting flames and sparks, the curls of smoke, that float up and out from the chimney. Each evening we have a little fire while we sit and read and the room grows cozy and warm.

A question about this wood we gather on the beach. I'm always wondering where it comes from. A fishing boat? A large sailing vessel wrecked ages back? A small rowboat of recent vintage? The possibilities are unlimited and what a fertile field for the dreaming.

We waken mornings here to the sound of song sparrows in the pines and bayberry and always the mellow clear call of the

Bob-whites. Two definite notes and sometimes a third as introduction. (Just to set the key?) Along the roadside we surprise families of small quail that skitter out of sight into the honeysuckle and wild roses. Everywhere is beach plum, the hard little buds on their stalks like white beads on a string. They open out into feathery snow, a mist of white over the landscape. In a week or so the blush of pink tells us the flowers are fading and fruit is on the way. Come September all our friends here will be making beach plum jelly.

Myriads of goldfinches like sparks of sunlight were weaving through the junipers and honeysuckle around our house when we set forth with a pail and clam rake this morning. We walked along the beach toward the Mill Pond. Pine pollen had drifted across the water, and the tide had washed it up in creases of pale gold onto mounds of coarse tan strawlike seaweed. We kept passing tiny crabs, sun faded to pale pink or white, and tossed in among the tangled beach grass. On the sand lay a number of flat sponges in odd shapes with long, slim, tapering sponge fingers. Everywhere were blue mussels and scallop shells and an occasional vacated horseshoe crab shell.

Along the rim of the water was this marvelous stuff called spindrift, looking exactly like whipped-up egg whites tumbled on the wet sand. The breeze shivered it a little but it stayed together in interesting forms. It looked almost edible and think of the minerals of the sea! Bob said we'd probably get our mineral quota from the clams we were going to have tonight. True, the spindrift was rather sandy.

As we neared the clam bed we heard the music of the quail. The clear rich tone was now here in the beach grass, now there in the bayberry. And then came the high and plaintive calls of a pair of gulls at the water's edge—a yearning, longing sound it was as the two great birds splashed and swam apart and then together.

The wet dark-gray sand was perforated with countless clam holes, some large, some small. Occasionally a little jet of water would shoot up from a hole. Soon Bob, in his shorts, was kneeling down in the wetness, and I was digging in comfort on a pillow wrapped in a piece of plastic. Should

I be ashamed? I wasn't. I was quite content
—and dry!

First we loosen up the sand with the rake
near a number of large holes. Then I go
exploring with my bare hands, following a
surface clam hole down about six inches.
There my fingers encounter the edge of a
shell. Gradually working them around and
being careful not to break the shell I bring
out a firm wet clam, often with its long
brown neck stuck out, and always tinted
with different shades of blues and grays and
sometimes a rustiness. In digging clams you
absolutely ruin your hands, even nicking
them here and there. You get cricks in your
back, neck and knees, and I don't know
anything that's more fun! Probably it is
partly the treasure-hunt aspect! Then there
is always a great satisfaction in getting from
the wild, and for nothing, a complete and
delicious meal. Little by little the pail fills
until we have enough for supper for two.
Bob cleans them off and we head for home.
We would leave them the rest of the day in
the pail of salt water and by late afternoon
they would have washed themselves clean
of sand.

By supper time we had really worked up

an appetite. Just a little water in the big kettle, a nice hot burner and let them boil up twice, until the shells spring open. Dunk each one first in broth and then in melted butter and what is more ambrosial!

I am settled for the afternoon by the waters of the inlet on the soft warm sand, writing letters. I was writing to friends back in Tryon, to our overnight hosts on our drive up, and to others in far places. Bob has gone to town to buy yellow paint to give our boat a fresh coat. The tide is rushing in, rippling the water surface as the great body of sea pushes up Robert's Cove to the Mill Pond. How mysterious are these tides —tides that, along with time, wait for no man—that are never late—that never forget to rise and fall, and that you can set your clock by.

"Let's go fishing," I said one afternoon last week. "I feel just like it, don't you?"

But no, first we must consult the tide table.

"We can go tomorrow morning any time from ten to twelve, but not now at four P.M." Bob said.

The best fishing is an hour or so after

the tide has started in. The tide makes our plans, not we, and I like it this way.

Here before me, as I write my letters, moves the tide, never hurrying to catch up because it's always on time. Overhead flies a great blue heron while some little plovers are choosing tidbits of food from the water's edge. From the rose bushes at my back I hear song sparrows and warblers with their witchety-witchety music.

I have a modest and personal crusade that I'm working away on quietly and by myself. It has to do with writing letters—which today seems a lost art. We hear so much about improving communications. Here is a beautiful field for just that, between friends, between parents and children of any age. At the moment we are engaged in an amusing, heartwarming and thoroughly satisfying correspondence with two of our grandchildren, ages nine and eleven. It may be only two or three times a year that letters are exchanged but they mean a great deal. Since these children live in California, we are establishing a wonderful link and a warm relationship that is furthered whenever we meet.

We hear a lot about a supposed

generation gap, and the difficulty teenagers have in communicating with parents and vice versa. What a substantial bridge a few friendly and sharing letters can build over this supposed chasm. Wouldn't it be great if letter writing were taught in the schools!

One of my simple rules for the most satisfying kind of correspondence is to have the letter I'm answering at hand and refer to it. Nothing is more frustrating than pouring out at length your thoughts and ideas and making no reference to anything said in your friend's response. It's like dropping ideas into the depths of the sea.

Letters weave a fabric of deep and meaningful relationships and a sense of closeness to grown children and friends in other parts of the country or the world. And, conversely, you can have a real sense of separateness and loss if there are no letters exchanged between family members or friends who live far apart and seldom meet.

Letter writing is not only a pleasure for the receiver but for the writer as well. When I settle for an afternoon with pen and paper it is like a visit with each person I write. My pleasantly diversified correspondence is heartwarming to me and a vital part of my relationship with the people involved.

While I am rambling on to my friend at Lake Windermere, in England, I am there. I am in her little stone house or in her tiny greenhouse of sweet peas, or helping her scatter bread for the birds. We are on the terrace watching rainbows over the lake or maybe we are walking with our picnic lunches around Buttermere, or Grassmere, visiting Wordsworth's cottage or wandering through pastures of sheep, and climbing the stiles over stone walls. As I write, our visit there comes alive again.

When I am writing to our son and daughter in San Francisco I am there in the patio garden with the small children on bicycles and tricycles. I see again the swirling fog over Golden Gate Bridge. Maybe we are picnicking on Mount Tamalpais, or all of us are driving down the coast toward Big Sur.

When I start a letter to friends in Paris I am there, walking along the Seine at night, watching pinpricks of light on the arching bridges. Maybe I'm held in wonder before the Winged Victory in the Louvre, or in the

Renoir Room in the Jeu de Paume Museum where we have all been together. Or I may be standing spellbound in Chartres Cathedral. On one sunny afternoon on Cape Cod I can travel across the country or half way around the world. When later I seal up my letters, I have been far, far away. But now I come back and start supper, feeling a great pleasure in being at home again.

The most exciting letters of all to write and to receive are those that come or go out of the blue. Letters we write on the spur of the moment just because—. We may be thinking of someone and maybe appreciating them a little more than usual that day. Fifteen or thirty minutes of our time can give pleasure out of proportion to those minutes. Also, when a friend is traveling, how happy it makes him or her to find a warm, newsy letter waiting at a port of call.

When you have company for dinner and someone in the group writes a friendly thank you, how you enjoy this. Letters received in the hospital also bring real appreciation. Even more when you're home again and ostensibly cured but still a bit wobbly, outwardly and inwardly. Another kind of letter I love to write is when I've been recalling some special experience a friend and I have had together, a happy and gay incident we have shared. All such letters out of the blue are unnecessary, not part of custom or politeness or manners, and consequently the most satisfying of all to receive and to send.

The lilacs shed their last misty violet flowers and we were in a world of roses. Today the house is full of roses, pink rugosa roses and white ones. When we walk down on the beach the air is redolent with the fragrance and the plants are nearly hidden beneath enormous blooms with tufted yellow centers. They tell a lovely story about how the rugosa rose first came to Cape Cod. There was a ship from Japan sailing off shore bringing plants and other things from the Orient to America. In a great storm the vessel was wrecked along the coast of the Cape. The small rose bushes drifted ashore, miraculously took hold, survived and multiplied. Equally miraculously, some had settled and flourished in pure sand. We often find them at the edges of pine woods, along roadsides, on banks and in fields, but they seem especially fragrant and happy in sand and on the beach.

The flowers don't last long in the house but they're worth picking for the fragrance that spreads to every room. If I gather them in bud and float them in a bowl we have the pleasure of watching them open and observing how the individual blossom grows larger and larger until the moment when the petals fall and the yellow tufted centers stand alone among prickly green leaves.

While sheets of pink and white roses are everywhere on the shore, snowy daisies with bright gold centers are appearing in the sunny meadows and along roadsides. Picking daisies is as great a delight as picking violets was some weeks back. I enjoy gathering them for ourselves and for friends. On the dining table is a large bouquet of these much-loved flowers, and lavender, clover soft to touch and fragrant, and bayberry. Together all these compose into a mini-meadow complete with meadow-grass-in-the-sun smell.

Happiness can come a little at a time and welcome is the kind that sweeps over us in complete surprise at some very ordinary moment. Thus it was with me this morning. I was settled on the front porch reveling in the sunshine, the distant cries of the gulls and the honeysuckle scent mingled with the fresh salt air. Before me were the red geraniums, dazzling really—each plant covered with blossoms large as grapefruit. The bank up to the dirt road was a mass of wild pink roses. I was eating black cherries, and embroidering white daisies with gold centers on blue plissé napkins—hostess presents for when we leave.

The sound of Bob's axe came from the other side of the house. He was cutting driftwood for the fire tonight. All of a sudden there flowed through me a beautiful feeling of complete content. There's something about wood cutting that seems as beneficent an occupation as making bread—and what a comfortable sound! How cheerful my daisies, how pleasantly warm the sun, how delicious the cherries!

There are so many different kinds of happiness. There is happiness that we seek and find. Happiness that we set the stage for by planning and organizing the things we like to do or places we like to go or friends we like to be with. There is the happiness that comes when life presents us with a day full of interesting and chosen activities. But I really think best of all are the moments that drift over us when we least expect them. A quiet mind and an open heart usually create the climate in which these times are most likely to appear.

I've never been exactly sure what a day made in heaven would be like but I suspect today would qualify. It was still and quiet and sunny. We were walking along the sand and through the marsh grass, carrying oarlocks, oars, and cushions. The tide was dead low, and I love that pungent smell of low tide. What is it? A mingling of mud and fish, and old rope, and saltiness, and wet grass, and more—.

The Mill Pond is a mirror. Our freshly painted yellow boat with the gray sea horse I put on the stern awaits. Anchor and rope trail fringes of stringy black seaweed. The clams deep under the mud send up greetings—an occasional squirt. Periwinkles are everywhere, barnacles on the rocks, and lying on the shore dark, mustardy-colored seaweed, shiny wet and with firm little round bubbles. Just under the water surface here is a cluster of mussels tangled in a wisp of seaweed. The pebbles, shells and seaweed are glossy and always a deeper color where wet.

In the yellow boat I feel a little as if we are traveling in a sunbeam. The blue water ruffles up as the oars dip in and out. We are leaving a wake, a great "V" in a pond still as glass. Two auxiliary "V's" form where the oars have been moving. The sun is warm, the air is still, and a single arctic tern with orange feet and bill flying overhead is silhouetted against blue sky. Over the side of the boat I watch the wavering grasses below the water surface. Here is one floating tuft, complete with roots, looking for a new home. How quiet it is not having a motor; the natural sounds and our leisurely pace are delicious to experience. We listen to the slap of water against the prow and the swish of oars. There's nowhere you can be more relaxed and removed from the world than out in a small slow-moving rowboat.

Looking down into the water I catch a

glimpse of a jellyfish, and another. Bob stops rowing and we watch one of these small creatures of the sea. It is shaped like an inverted transparent soup bowl. It's fascinating to see it undulating through the water. It is composed of four geometric circles on what would be the bottom of the soup bowl. There are four veil-like fins inside the "bowl" which move gracefully as it slides along under the water. The word jellyfish has a sort of questionable connotation. People speak of some individual being spineless as a jellyfish. I don't believe I'll want to say that again, for this wisp of submarine life is a miracle of wonder—ephemeral, translucent, nothing really and yet a spark of living. If you took it out of water I believe it would be literally nothing. For a few moments we watched it in its own element, graceful, mysterious, something to awe you as it moves through the water. Now, after resting a moment among the leaves of some seaweed, it passes out of sight into the shadows of the deep.

We have reached the end of the Mill Pond and are entering a narrow, shallow channel to a second and very small pond. We scrape bottom here and there but are just able to move ahead. This little pond, a sort of annex, is bordered with pine, and from its shore rises a hill of pine. As Bob rows gently along we are both remembering and reminding each other.

All those summers here when our children were little have filled the area with nostalgic memories. The hill of pines toward which Bob is rowing is where the great blue heron used to nest and we and the children would wander there, always hoping to find a nest or see young birds. Then there was the night that Bob and our two sons, Bob and Tim, camped in a tent on the shore of the Mill Pond. The boys must have been about nine and ten and it was a great occasion and a terrific adventure. Joan, a couple of years older, and with a delicious streak of mischief in her, gathered a few of her friends and an ancient and clanking chain from somewhere. When the men of the family were supposedly asleep, the girls tiptoed along the beach, wrapped in sheets and clanking the chain, thereby enhancing, of course, the whole evening and experience. We were laughing now to remember this and other happenings, other days, and other years.

Bob skillfully maneuvered the boat up to a large tuft of beach grass. We anchored there. What an enchanted spot—quiet except for an occasional bird calling. A small house roof or chimney visible in the distance, otherwise greenery, water and sky, solitude. The seaweed here along the water's edge is in tones of gray where it is dry and dead and bouncy to walk on, and mustardy-brown where it is live and wet. Walking up from the shore we found an old wood road that wandered through the pines. The earth underfoot was soft and resilient. Sun and shadows flickered over the red pine-needle floor. And here was poison ivy! The ominous vine was everywhere. We had to watch, to look, and step aside. Isn't there always a little something on our paths wherever we are that we need to be careful of and avoid? Today, because we are watching and cautious, we discover all sorts of treasures. Oak leaves budding deep pink on a tiny seedling tree. A single black feather. Does this belong to the blackcrowned night heron? And now I am crushing a sprig of new young bayberry leaves for fragrance. The first crush in my fingers is the most pungent. In moments the scent changes and becomes less appealing. Everywhere yellow pine pollen falls, dusting the leaves where we walk along.

And now we emerge into a magic glade, a locust grove filled with the music of birds. A small Cape Cod house stands in the center, very old and perfect. We remember this house from years back and wonder who lives in it now. There used to be a golden chain tree here and it would be blooming now, but where is it? Did it die? The garage is open so someone lives here but for the moment is away. I settle down in the sun on the doorstep made of half an old millstone. I was wishing the people would come home so we could tell them how much we admire their little house. Bob wanders down the drive to see where we are located. I really didn't care—didn't want to be located anywhere—because this was a different world and I wanted to keep it so for just a few minutes. From the doorstep I looked beyond a little garden toward a tiny pond covered with lily pads; the sun was beneficiently warm; a small and comfortable toad hopped in the grass at my feet. When Bob came back we began to envision the people who lived here. What would they be like? A retired couple, maybe?

"There's a little chimney on the roof of a small shed back there," said Bob. "There must be a man who has a shop where he likes to work in cold weather."

We both sat awhile and imagined and dreamed. No one appeared and pretty soon we climbed back up over the hill and rowed slowly and lazily across both ponds to home.

It was a quiet and gentle sunny morning after three days of wind and storm. Bob and I were walking barefoot along the sand on the outer beach. Down at the water's edge great rollers were pounding the shore. They still held in them elements of the storm. We must shout to hear each other. Perhaps it is better to be silent and listen to messages from the sea. Now a great crash and then the swish of waves that shape into foaming white scallops on the sand. Water comes up over our feet, icy cold. Now it's on our ankles and an occasional curl of wetness dashes against our knees and sends us running back. I feel the power of the ocean running through me, to my fingertips and to the ends of my hair. The roar of these giant breakers seems to play on every nerve. For a moment I am the waves and the waves are me.

We walk along the sand, mostly we're not really thinking, purely feeling, listening, receiving, being, merging with these forces of nature.

The air is fragrant with the sea, the salty tang instinctively causes me to breathe deeply, breathe loosely, and stretch inside. A wonderful sense of freedom fills me as the waves wash over my feet and the soft sand scrunches between bare toes. I watch Bob making footprints ahead of me in the sand. After him a wave smooths them away. Following him I make a new set and behind me the next wave washes the sand smooth again. Behind us both it is as if we had not been there, only smooth sand and sea, sound and fragrance.

The sea is blue, the sky is blue, and now the very air is blue with a blueness that permeates and fills us even as the sound of the rollers encompasses us.

Walking along we look up the shoreline. The beach is patterned by waves. Advancing and receding they have etched the silhouettes of great mountain ranges on the sand. Beneath my feet on the slope of the beach are the volcanoes of Guatemala, the ranges of the Alps, the Blue Ridge, and the Smokies, all drawn by the sea. Here they are, peak after peak, rough, rugged, steep and majestic, all the mountains we've known and loved outlined clearly in the sand.

I remember some years ago, when in our favorite little mile-high village of St. Luc, surrounded by the Alps, on certain mornings the valley below was bathed in clouds of mist. Mountains rose up out of this sea of whiteness as it moved and drifted back and forth until gradually the warming sun melted it away. But for a few moments before the white vapors disappeared, the sea was there in those mountain mists complete with breakers and snowy tossing foam.

While the mountains speak of the sea, the sea echoes the rolling ranges. The one area hints of the other. There is in each of us that of both mountains and sea and what they symbolize. Surely the mountains are for strength, endurance, the ability to take what comes and weather it, to hold fast. There is foreverness in mountains.

The sea is for feelings, emotions, the ability to change, adapt, flow around obstacles, to move and go places.

Don't we all need the qualities of both?

Our month of June is blissfully sliding by, one day melting into the next. Each one is a beautiful merging of sand and sea, blue sky and birds, marvelous scents and myriads of flowers, interesting sights and sounds and wanderings by car to different parts of the Cape. Joan came for a visit to share in our experience. Much of our fun up here, both before Joan came and afterward, centers along the shore, fishing for flounder in silence in the still, still Mill Pond. Never catching any—not caring— keeping the refrigerator always stocked with the most horrendous sea worms for bait just in case.

How delightful was the occasion of eating our annual lobsters, the three of us. On the outer beach we flew our kite from a dune of waving beach grass, taking turns holding the string while we watched the flowing motions of the great Japanese kite, silver and twenty feet long. Always eager to be airborne, it would tug and pull at the line as it soared as high as we'd let it. The silver catches the sun and reflects it back in brilliant sparkles while the kite weaves and turns and ripples in the breeze. There's something about flying a kite that is strangely akin to fishing. In our little boat, as I hold the line over the edge, I relate to the depths of the sea in an intimate sort of way. I feel the movement of the water down deep as it comes to me through the slight vibration of the line. Likewise, when holding the string of a kite, you are in touch with yet another and different dimension, this time the air above. Through the string in your hand you feel the tempo and force of high-up air currents as they lift and carry the kite aloft and keep it there.

Mingled with all these peak moments we have 'coons that come with the dawn and toss the garbage cans around among themselves, rolling them hither and yon. Bob is in a constant battle with them. He firmly ties the tops on, but in spite of this, often in the morning the grass is strewn with clam shells and chicken bones and grapefruit rinds. He became quite creative in evolving better and stronger knots. He really thought he had them conquered when yesterday one ate through the bottom of a garbage can and there was a dismaying collection of food remnants scattered far and wide. Eventually a sturdy new can and special kind of knots for the top seemed to have solved 'coons—except for one that galumps up and over the roof each night. It seems to do no harm. It must like to watch the moon rise from high up. When raccoons are not being destructive they are rather attractive creatures. Are the raccoons and poison ivy in our lives just to keep us alert, resourceful and stimulated to creative action?

But we forget them in wandering down where terns nest among the dunes. Fortunately a whole section of beach where these birds breed is marked off and no beach cars or people are permitted. But the terns don't always know where the boundaries are.

Here in a depression in the sand just outside the specified area, and right where we are walking, are three eggs—round and speckled, beautiful in shape. Nearby is another nest with one egg, and over there are two. All the while overhead the frantic terns wheel and dive. They don't want us here and I can't blame them.

Please, I tell them in my mind, we walk carefully and won't hurt or disturb. Let us look, let us briefly step into your so different world, your world of natural ways and instincts, that weaves a course through our more complicated and peopled world.

The sun shines warm on the eggs, helping to hatch them. The gulls call and fly overhead. And here is a very newly hatched chick nestled close to a piece of gray driftwood. The breeze gently ruffles its soft down. This little scrap of beginning life blinks at us sleepily and we walk quietly away. The sound of the terns fades in the distances. How relieved their calls—no more harsh squawks—now that we are leaving their private area.

One day we were on the beach in the fog. The bluff had disappeared. It was as if it and all the small houses on top did not exist. We had slipped out of our peopled world. The whole beach was hidden except just where we walked. A great flock of gulls flew up to circle around us disturbing mortals, and then they settled behind us as we moved along. When they soared they disappeared into fog and then appeared again.

This world of fog creates a quiet and blue-gray privacy in which we move. A single white gull feather is blowing over the sand, leading us on. A tangle of brown-green ribbon seaweed lies at our feet, pointing the way. We cannot see ahead where our path leads, nor where we have been by looking backward, but only where we are. As we move forward the way unfolds before us, a little stretch at a time, just what we need and no more.

Two small sandpipers speed over the beach as though on wheels; their stiff little legs move so fast we can scarcely see them.

Our last afternoon on the beach and a sunny one! Where gulls have been their tracks have crisscrossed, creating interesting patterns in the sand. The tracks of the sandpipers are little nubs of sand pushed this way and that. Bob stoops to pick up a shell, a smooth round white stone.

"A feeling stone?" I ask him.

"Yes." He hands it to me. I curve my fingers around its firm smoothness and hold it a minute. A stone from the beach in your hand has a special cool, firm quality. It brings a sense of the foreverness that it has taken to assume this shape and size. I pass the stone back to Bob, and he slips it into his pocket. The beach abounds in shells and stones—all shapes and sizes and colors —yellow, blue-gray and pure white. In today's brilliant sunlight even the smallest pebbles cast shadows, tiny blue shadows sharp-tipped like pencil points. The larger stones cast larger shadows and the broken shells reflect jagged shapes of blue on the soft white sand.

Our walk was almost a quiet one—how little we needed to say. How little needs to be said here. The need is more to listen than to speak as it often is when on the beach.

I like the Zen saying:

Those who know don't speak,
Those who speak don't know.

I don't know that I know or what I know,

but I do enjoy silences, when I'm alone, when I'm with another person, and especially when walking with Bob. Certain people are better than others to be quiet with. Some cannot be quiet at all and what a lot they miss. With Bob, silences are never empty but moments of fullness. There is so much to take in that words could find no place. We are already filled to overflowing with feelings and responses to our surroundings. While we listen I am absorbing like a dry sponge under water. I want to be quiet and continue to receive. I am reminded of a quotation from Isaiah:

In returning and rest you shall be
    saved;
in quietness and in trust shall be your
    strength.

The sun slips lower and lower. A single fisherman packs up his rod and reel and moves off. We are alone with the sea, the dunes, the gulls and the sandpipers. Birds are calling, a high and lonely sound when you are lonely, a warm and friendly sound when you are not. We scrunch along in cooling wet sand.

161

The day is ending and so is our month at the shore.

Back at the Flutery I sweep the porch, wanting to leave things neat and clean for the tenants. But I do not lose the ocean. The rhythm of breaking waves is with me, in my bones and spirit as I stir about cleaning things up and getting supper. Surely I am moving more slowly and easily for all motion seems effortless. Don't we catch the rhythms of nature when we open and expose ourselves to them? Tonight we shall have our last driftwood fire. A beautiful month of flowers and fragrances, salt air and gulls, wood smoke in the night, and always the sea and what it brings.

7

July Is a Rain Forest

AFTER the vastness of blue skies, blue sea, and lines horizontal, what a difference to be back in a green and vertical world. The mountains of Tryon are hazy but their lines are all upward. The perpendiculars of tree trunks, pines, tall slim tulip trees, sourwoods, the liquid amber, and the great white oak lead the vision up and up in contrast to the Cape's wide vistas stretching to the far horizon. Out of the sparse windstunted vegetation of the Cape into the rich lush greenness of Tryon. Such a change, and yet a welcome one. How pleased we were at the first sight of the mountains and, as we turned into our drive, the last two beautiful huge magnolia blossoms, snowy white and pristine, waiting to greet us.

We've had our holiday, our distant trip, our visits in the North. A time of old friends and new ideas, new directions, stimulating conversations. The past ten days of wandering and visiting and living out of suitcases was exactly long enough. Now we are happy to be back where our roots now reach deeply down, and to be settling within our own four walls, with our garden, with our friends and neighbors. We've taken in so much that is thought-provoking and exciting, we want now an interlude of absorbing and digesting, and of appreciating the quiet beauty that is Tryon in the summer.

Everywhere crepe myrtle is opening, deep pink tossing plumes over the landscape. The fragrance of gardenias rises through warm misty air. The small trailing gardenia plant with its shiny green leaves is covered with pure white, deeply scented flowers and the bushes of the larger varieties are also masses of blossoms. Petunias are big as saucers. Otherwise the garden is cool green, a mixture of interesting textures, and a variety of forms and shapes. Here and there a tiny pink patience flower brightens a shady corner. And that yucca plant with its blue-green needle-sharp leaves? Is it getting out of hand? It has grown enormously while we were away and reaches out well into the path to remind us, rather uncomfortably, of its presence.

Here at home we have lost the sky and the clear starry nights we lived with on the shore. Instead we have a canopy of deep green leaves, the largest leaves I've ever seen. We may see only an occasional star, but no matter, we know they are all there. To remind us of this, myriads of starry fireflies begin their darting dances at dusk. Dazzling about they catch in the screens, pausing briefly there while their pulsing light reminds us once again of the mysterious and different worlds that interpenetrate our own. Another of these worlds is inhabited by the cicadas, those evening insects that, in a variety of tunes and rhythms, sing us to sleep. They seem to speak and answer each other on and on, beginning at dark and continuing their chant until just before dawn.

One evening we were sitting on the terrace with Homer watching the flickering light of the Japanese stone lantern and listening to these creatures of the night.

"Do you know," Homer said, "if you

knock on the trunk of a tree where they are they stop singing on the instant?"

Immediately I rose and wandered about knocking on nearby trees.

"You must make it a definite and firm knock," our neighbor added.

"They always seem to be in the tree just beyond," I replied, firming up my knock. "Where are they, anyway?"

After our guest left I walked toward the woodland path. Sounds are everywhere, but never seemingly anywhere specific, never in the tree at my side. Just to be friendly I tapped a little here and there indiscriminatingly. I didn't want to frighten these musicians: only to communicate some way, to let them know I am here and listening.

At the end of the house the tomatoes are about eight feet tall! They have ascended to the tip of the poles and beyond and now have started down again. How sweetscented the foliage is to touch, or even to walk past. In the early morning you can see the pungent drops of scent oil, pinpricks of moisture on the deeply indented leaves. In among these are promising green fruit. But actually not much fruit for the amount of greenery. Not enough sun, perhaps? We drive over to Mrs. Jennings's garden our first afternoon home and return with armfuls of fresh lettuces with the earth still clinging to the roots, bright red vine-ripened tomatoes, long slim cucumbers, just-picked sweet corn, beans and squashes. All are filled with "sun power" as the mountain people call it because they are gathered after the sun has been shining on them for several hours. Vegetables picked in the early, early morning before sunup have moon and star power in them, we are told! So we can't lose.

We revel in this garden produce, fresh from the soil, bringing us not only the unrivaled flavor of just-harvested vegetables, sun, moon and star power from the heavens above, but nutrients of the earth. We consider our own tomatoes, deeply shaded with maybe only two or three hours of sun a day, and we wonder. In the spring we *had* to plant. An urge not to be denied had compelled us. Is it going to be worth it? Maybe so, just for the fragrance of the plant, and the look of the large green fruits, even if there aren't so many. They hang there taller than we are and a good long reach away.

We turn from the tomatoes to our fig tree covered with little green figs, firm and hard but redolent of future possibilities.

"Hush," we tell each other, admiring what will be our first home-grown fruit, "Lest the birds hear our enthusiasm and come to investigate."

So far they haven't discovered these figs. We counted thirty-four. The tree grows out by the road in good sun for half a day at least. Now at long last we shall have figs for breakfast, lunch and dinner, figs and honey and cream; yes, nice thick cream for the occasion.

Now that we are back, nearly every day we find ourselves drifting about in the clear blue-green pool at Mimosa Inn where the water is warm and caressing. What a wonderful feeling of cool relaxation in swimming back and forth from one end of the pool to the other! And all the while the scent of the mimosa flowers from the great spreading trees overhead drifts down. Every blossom is a white powderpuff, pink-dipped. Some of the blossoms fall down and float on the water.

These days remind me of visits to the rain forests in the banana countries of Honduras and Guatemala. Tryon this summer is strangely akin to these tropical areas. Lots of rain falls. Sixty inches a year any year, and more than that this year if it continues as it has so far. Certain days here it may rain many times, possibly a light shower but perhaps several inches in an afternoon or in an hour or two. The sun frequently emerges between downpours, and you see its beams filtering through a steaminess. Were I a poet I would compose a sonnet to this hazy filtering sunlight. The terrace is a-sparkle with the sun's light and brilliance as it sifts through the trees. Then, as a small breeze stirs, shadows move gently in a sort of dance over the bricks.

We like living in a woods. We enjoy the quiet and silence of trees, the liquid amber, whose name I love to slide over my tongue, all kinds of oaks—the white oak, chestnut oak, Spanish oak. The black gum, the giant and dignified tulip tree. We have them all including the sassafras with those amusing mitten-shaped leaves.

The wet and heavy growing quality that hangs in the air here is not unpleasant actually, but a quality that takes a little getting used to, since we never experienced it in New England. The moist earthiness seems to relate you to the soil and as you walk along the garden path and out by the tomatoes and figs you can almost feel things burgeoning.

The hot damp air sometimes seems to press down on you with a weight. In town the sidewalks feel hot through shoe soles. We are aware of a delicious lethargy spreading over us. It is more important to swing on the gate than to go about anything briskly and efficiently. Who wants to be perky in July when you can drift about in blue pool water, watch fireflies at night, read a favorite novel by the brook as you listen to the water ripple, and feel the damp earth on your hands while in the fresh early morning you pull a lazy weed or two.

It's no wonder Southerners move with a slow and gracious rhythm. How wise they are. Occasionally we, from the North, forget this and find ourselves stirring around briskly, only to be aware all of a sudden of heat, heat, and HEAT. Abruptly we stop and permit the slow leisurely way again to flow over us. We remember where we are, we relax, we move slowly, and consequently we feel different and better. In the late afternoons on the terrace we sip homemade lemonade and watch the last rays of the sun catching the tips of the sourwood across the street. Everywhere in the area the sourwoods are coming into full flower and they are beautiful—a tossing fringe of whiteness. The blossoms open in drooping racemes of waxy white bell-shaped florets filling the air with fragrance and inviting all the honeybees in the neighborhood. The mountain people call these blossoms "angel-fingers," and often the tree is known as the "lily-of-the-valley-tree." Each single flower stalk in the cluster suggests this namesake.

The sourwood tree is famed in our area because of the choiceness of the honey the bees gather from it. It is a favorite tree for other reasons too. The long, narrow glossy leaves turn a vivid scarlet in the fall and paint the coves and mountainsides with a dazzling hue. We treasure the sourwoods on our place. The mountain people years back prized these trees because they often had crooked or curved trunks which made perfect sled runners. They also used the wood for tool handles and bedposts. But they never made a fire with it for it was very bad luck to burn it and disaster might descend upon the household! If a native child had asthma the father would cut a limb the exact height of the child and lay it beneath the doorstep. By the time the child's height exceeded the length of the stick the asthma would have vanished.

Speaking of honey, bees are a vital part of these lazy summer days; and standing under the sourwoods we hear them busily and pleasantly humming above. The country people say that if you would like to find a bee tree to get wild honey, wander out in the wooded areas on some hot night and listen. The bees fan the honey to keep it cool and you can hear an almost purring sound from the ground below. There you know is a treasure and the bees are guarding it as they fan it with their wings.

One morning we wakened to crisp clear coolness. Gone was the steam and the mist and the air was fresh and alive with the smell of cool mountains.

"This is the way it usually is in the summer." So Mr. Cowan in the market tells us, while we are selecting his delectable melons and blueberries. "This is real Tryon weather."

But I suspect Mr. Cowan, like us at heart, appreciates both kinds of weather and sees how they complement each other. For two days we are cool, eating all our meals on the porch and looking out into the treetops. I make friends again with the garden, down on my hands and knees, weeding along the path, or pruning, or tying things up against the fence—Bob on one side of it and me on the other.

In Tryon they say that when you start a new garden the first year everything sleeps; the second year it creeps; the third year it leaps. We are in our third year and weeding consists of making a decision every few inches. What plant do I want to grow in this spot—for here are three all on top of each other. For example, an azalea has crept through the fence to crowd a primrose that was planted there originally; a long streamer of climbing hydrangea is trying to obliterate the first two. And inching over toward the same beset primrose are runners of the foam flower all bound up in some ivy. Which has the right of way? Those cool mornings I was out early before breakfast, trimming, pruning and shaping. And observing. A large plant of foam flower could be moved and would grow down by the brook on the bank along the water's edge. I left some where it was and took a great piece of it down the path to the water. With the ample rainfall we can transplant all summer long. Piled here and there among the primroses are the empty dried shells of dozens of snails telling us how well the slug bait works.

One early morning Bob and I were gardening together, pulling up a bushel of ajuga, mostly from the brick terrace. Strangely enough ajuga loves to grow among the bricks. We also dug up extra perennial begonias, ivy and myrtle, and left them all on wet newspapers in the shade for Homer. Bob came over to where I was weeding and handed me a four-leaf clover that he just picked. Good things ahead?

A wise and well-loved friend recently gave me five rules.

"Include all of these in each day," she said, "and see what happens."

1. Do one thoughtful thing for someone else.
2. Do an "ought-to-do" you've been putting off because you don't much like it, something you don't really want to do but should.
3. Don't speak aloud about a single one of your miseries or problems.
4. Do something you simply love to do, something that purely fills your spirit and heart with joy and delight. The less "worthwhile" the better—the crazier and more purposeless, the better. This is the most important rule of all!
5. At night, review the day from the point of view of your higher self. How did you do? Is there anything you might have done differently and better? What are you especially pleased with that occurred as a result of these attitudes and actions? Are there any subsequent events that these may have led to?

A favorite Emerson quote of mine: "A man is what he is thinking all day long."

A small miracle is occurring outside under the holly bush growing against the house.

In three empty Campbell soup cans I've a batch of gardenia cuttings. Recently a friend suggested we come over and take cuttings from her large bush that was covered with blooms. I pruned off about ten six-inch stalks, trimmed off the lower leaves, and snipped away the ends of the upper ones. Next I slit with scissors, lengthwise, the bottom end of each stem. I put about four inches of stem under water (not even bothering with Rootone, good as it is), set them in the shade and under the eaves where rain cannot beat down. A week ago I did this, and now this morning I went out to change the water. Tiny white rootlets are visible on all the wet blackened stems. Some are white threads in clusters a quarter of an inch long; others are as yet mere white dots of life energy all up and down the stem and ready to emerge. This is terribly exciting!

Here at the end of each small cutting I had taken from the main plant is enough life and vitality to produce another bush! Many times a day I find myself thinking with delight of what is happening out there under the holly in those soup cans.

A garden is a place for miracles—every few days a new one.

How much vitality lingers in a small cut zinnia flower and stem. One rests on the kitchen window sill in a tiny vase. I set the blossom facing the room yesterday. It was still facing the room this morning, but now, a couple of hours later, I stepped into the kitchen and it has turned its head and stem around to face outdoors! I couldn't believe it, but it was true. I have observed that tulips in water have a way of rearranging themselves. The zinnias in a bouquet in the center of the dining table have moved about a little, their stalks developing fascinating curves. Amazing to me that after a flower is cut from its plant, its source of life and energy, it still has enough vitality to stir and literally move from here to there.

And so the month slides by. We eat breakfast every morning on the porch and listen to the hum of wasps making long strings of red mud nests up under the eaves. We must spray them tonight when they are all in, we agree. But by then we are reading or listening to music and we forget. Neither of us much likes to kill anything anyhow.

The weight of moisture in the morning air melts ambition. Let's have an easy quiet day I decide as we eat our delicious local melon. Thus with the semitropical summer heat we are relaxing willy-nilly and glowing with the season. Here on the hillside the great oaks and tulip trees breathe out their life-giving oxygen through the warm air. How fortunate we are not to be near a city. We read of pollution and crowding. Here it may be warm but we always have the cool sound of the running stream, and the freshness of the surrounding woodland.

At night there is the sound of the frogs in the street puddle across the way. We love these frogs. When we have a dry few days the puddle disappears. Where do the frogs go? Do they wait under some nearby tree or bush, hovering about and anticipating the next rain so they can gather again and sing their lovely nightly songs? Long after we are in bed we still listen to them.

Occasionally I half wake around five-thirty to hear the distant train whistle through the valley, a long and hauntingly lonely sound. And I remember our honeymoon, and that sound so connected with those two weeks in Asheville lots of years ago, and I begin to muse on all that has happened since.

A valuable insight came to me recently on a long drive alone. I love driving, and all the sights and sounds and smells encountered. Watching the landscape at whatever season is a real pleasure. When you drive alone your thoughts run all over the place—the past, present, future, friends, places, books, everything. To my surprise I discovered that after driving along in a cheerful and happy mood for a few hours my thoughts would turn into a negative vein. At first this puzzled me because I was enormously happy and having a wonderful time. But the answer was simple. I was tired. When the negative appeared I would stop for a short walk and a drink of juice, or a meal, or I'd draw off the road and stretch out in the car for a brief relax. Usually after such a break I'd be free from the negative. If I wasn't, I knew I had driven far enough for that day. When it happened about three in the afternoon as it often did, my negative streak usually stayed with me until I did stop.

It has since become my firm belief that, basically, people are positive in their thinking, and are inherently kindly. That when they are their true selves and all is well with them they just naturally think constructively. Mostly it is when we are a little off the track ourselves that we take out after another and this can be due to fatigue which brings on fear, apprehensions, general uneasiness, and disapproval.

Today I have discovered that when I find myself in a negative swing it is because I am tired. Something needs changing. Somewhere I am off the beam. The need is to reassess and take a better look at just where I am and what I am doing. There is some fault in my chosen path or direction. Somewhere I have gone astray. This is often because I have become involved in too many different and varied activities. Mainly just too many. I need an interlude alone to sort out the real and significant from the unimportant. I take off a day or two, remain quietly at home, simplify meals, and if I can arrange it, stay in bed. I get up and get meals but remain in bed the rest of the time, reading, writing letters, sewing, dozing, just lying there looking out the window. This way I find my center again, and balance back. Fears and apprehensions vanish. I no longer have to, with effort, yank and pull my thoughts back to positive as I do if I try to keep up and doing. They just naturally flow into a positive vein.

One day Helen arrived in her white station wagon. Doesn't each of our friends represent a different world in us, a world that comes alive only in that particular friendship? This is the way it is with Helen. Each year she comes for a couple of weeks, and while she is here Bob and I explore together the very special realms which we are never able to enter into in quite the same way without her.

She always arrives with armloads of presents. This year there was home-smoked dried beef, goat's milk yogurt, a special and heavenly granola, herb tea, and her recent favorite books to share; books that she thought we'd like, and a marvelous organic cookbook for me.

She also brought her bicycle and each day before breakfast she would explore our mountain roads.

We are a most compatible threesome as we wander around sharing our guest with friends and having her alone. Helen loves swimming as much as we do, and we go each day to the Mimosa Inn.

One of our special joys here in Tryon is having guests from the North come and visit. To celebrate Helen, we decided to have a party.

Japanese lanterns in all colors are strung along a wire from the corner of the carport to the Spanish oak and then onto the house, creating two sides of a triangle, the front of the house being the third side. The little Japanese stone lantern has a sturdy candle inside. Guests are coming for a buffet supper. Chicken salad, celery, olives, carrots, bran muffins and coconut cake—and seventeen people. Our largest party since we arrived—a truly gala affair.

Far more than can fit into our house; actually far more than the number of chairs we have, silver and such. But friends have loaned things. Everyone knew everyone and some sat on the floor.

We'd asked people to bring a favorite poem or bit of prose and be prepared to read their choice, and comment. Each person's selection was so different from that of his neighbor. We ranged from Robert Frost to Kahlil Gibran. From the Bible to Emerson. It was a sort of enchanted evening and it cooled off so we could all move out on the terrace. The exotic Oriental touch of the old-fashioned Japanese lanterns and their flickering candles put everyone in a dreamy mood. Here and there through the foliage an occasional star twinkled down. The cicadas provided music for the party and in addition there was the deep base sound of our frogs in the puddle across the way. Fireflies darted about the azalea and holly bushes. Everyone was caught by the same mood of magic in such a setting, and the whole evening was one of warmth and response to one another. The final note was all of us standing in a circle, linking arms and singing favorite songs.

After the winking lights of the cars disappeared down the road into the darkness, the three of us sat on the terrace, watching the Japanese lanterns and calming down before going to bed. It was stimulating, a large group of congenial friends like this, and the conversation thought-provoking and exciting. After everyone had gone we welcomed that cooling-off period.

Helen's entire visit was one of the best. Among all the things she crowded into her station wagon was her newly acquired juicer and in it she created for us the delectable flavor of carrot, celery, beet, and apple juice with a touch of parsley and cucumber. And now we have ordered a juicer of our own.

An interlude of special meaning came after supper on Helen's last night. We drove up the mountain to watch the sunset, the top down, and we three together in the front seat. How deliciously cool it was. Up and up the car climbed, swinging around the curves on the mountain road, gaining in height and vistas at every bend. We must catch our views in brief glimpses through lush greenery, here a small gap and there another. And now on one side we can see toward the far off ranges, while on the other the eye travels down into the blueness of the great rolling Piedmont.

It was early for the sunset so we drove on up the mountain road bordered with Queen Anne's lace, wild phlox and clusters of tall, single golden glow blossoms. Here was a narrow wood road leading off through trees to who knew where. We left the car and wandered down the road, watching the sun slip lower and lower. A kind of predusk golden light spread over the western heavens. Up here is lots of sky. Farther along the dirt lane we suddenly saw them, the arching branches that in May had been covered with misty white flowers. Now they were all but hidden beneath ripening blackberries. Some were pale green, some red, and many rich purple-black. Seedy and rather sour they were, but sun-warmed and with a wild strong tang that was mountains in essence. We tasted a few and moved on to an open clearing of blueberries. These were ripe and sweet and we ate our fill. Beyond the blueberries stood tall white blossoms and more golden glow. I picked a great armful of flowers and we walked back to the car and drove back down to our favorite sunset-viewing spot. Here we parked and watched range after range of Blue Ridge mountains, blue veils, soft and folding, one beyond the other. Their curving overlapping silhouettes had the quiet rhythm of gentle music. Above them great rolling clouds and a red glow merged, constantly changing shape. The red glow gathered itself into a triangular form, an obvious arrow, pointing north, indicating Helen's direction on the morrow. The arrow changed into a red fox curled round upon itself with a large flowing tail. Then up there in the heavens we recognized a galloping horse, mane and tail tossing. And now bits of grayness were breaking through the red shapes from behind and the colors began to dim fast.

Next morning the world was all practical. Bob was getting the ice for Helen's cooler —Did you remember the sandwiches? Where will you put the fruit juice? The melons, the peaches? And the bicycle— Will it fit in? And the gardenia cuttings? Oh yes, these can go between the books and the juicer!

After fond farewells, Helen drove off and the white car, well loaded, disappeared around the bend. We were lonely and yet full. Something new had been added. Something deep had been stirred and quickened. There was a fresh aliveness and sense of creativity in the air—or was it within us?

After Helen left we weeded the garden. How lush and abundant everything has become. And each day we have more tomatoes turning pink and then red. We keep discovering more fruit well hidden down amongst the burgeoning foliage. We've no more questions about growing tomatoes. How could we not—even in this semishade?

8

August—A Time of Gathering In

AS a child I recall Sunday mornings, standing in our little country church singing hymns—and one of my favorites was "Bringing in the Sheaves." I especially remember the refrain "And we shall come rejoicing, bringing in the sheaves."

When I was very young and could not read, hearing the words sung around me I always thought they were not "bringing in the sheaves" but "three ate a cheese!" I used to puzzle over this and wonder which three. There was a lot of conversation about the Father, the Son and the Holy Ghost and, at the tender age of six, I used to ponder whether they were the three participating. But I didn't like to think of Jesus' mother being left out. Maybe she wasn't because how could a Holy Ghost eat cheese? I was rather hazy about what a Holy Ghost was but didn't think it was substantial enough to be wanting food. I always intended to ask my parents to explain these possibilities, but when the hour of "sitting still" in church was over I was ready to run off with my friends and I forgot.

At that youthful age, and growing up on a gentleman's farm—not a vast Kansas one —I never knew exactly what a sheaf was. This was mystifying. I had in my mind something about golden grain and I always envisioned columns of people of all ages from youngsters to the older generation and everyone in between. I used to imagine them all dancing along the road from the great fields to the barns. We had a barn and a hayloft so this was easy to picture. Each person carried armfuls of something dry and fragrant and surely golden. I could see them all, the women in colorful skirts and gay kerchiefs, singing and dancing, which to me was essential to rejoicing. So there we were. A complete scene.

This hymn to me expresses August in essence at any era.

There is a particular kind of rejoicing today as we "bring in the sheaves." They do not necessarily have to be golden sun-ripened wheat. These days we are all going slightly mad about canning, preserving, freezing—and the theme of the moment is peaches.

It has been interesting to follow the annual cycle of the orchards. In autumn we have admired the peach foliage, yellow with a warm glow almost like the peaches themselves. Next, the slim colorful leaves drift down to reveal the spreading shapes of bare trees through the winter; the first buds, little round pink-tipped nubs develop on twisted dark branches, and soon open into a pink foam of spring blossoms; and then the lush green leaves and hard little beginning-green fruits appear. Now the circle is complete as we see the trees heavy with large ripe peaches, weighing the branches down.

The squirrel in me is being thoroughly and continually satisfied at this season as every few days I carry down plastic bags or square containers, filled with a variety of produce, to arrange in our freezer depths. A freezer is a promise and I like that kind of promise. Surely these things we have tucked away will bring us not only their delicious flavors and pleasant memories but a goodly portion of that mysterious and exotic sun, moon, and star power that helped them to grow and ripen, and therefore must still lodge in all the produce! These are days of harvest and fullness and the richness of summer with nature and the earth giving and giving and we receiving.

One morning on the screened porch we were eating a delectable cranshaw melon that our neighbors had sent over the night before.

"Look," said Bob, sipping his coffee, "just look at that tulip tree there."

I looked. The leaves of the tulips here are enormous. And such a neat trim shape. You can readily see in the outline a suggestion of the form of tulip blossoms found in spring gardens.

"You see," Bob went on, biting into a piece of toast, "all the leaves the tulip produces are tulip leaves, and there mingling branches with it stands a maple, but in spite of this it never produces a leaf shaped like a maple. And the maple on the other hand maintains its maple pattern in every leaf it hangs on the twigs. And there is the oak, too. Now wouldn't you think," he said seriously, "that one would perhaps be influenced by the other? That sometimes the tulip might get confused and make a maple or oak-shaped leaf? But no, each stays with its own form, each has its own integrity. Remarkable!"

I look over at my husband. He is a solid down-to-earth person, but now and again he has these delightful flights of fantasy. As we munched the buttered toast I gazed at the trees just there beyond the screening. Bob's idea is intriguing on all levels! Every tree is infallible, knows its own, and stays with it. Would I were always as certain about what is my own, about what is me, and not thrown off-base, swayed, or influenced by an unfamiliar point of view or environment.

All month our figs have been ripening. We have watched them change from hard greenness to a reddish tint and felt their softness develop. And then came the great day when we picked our first few and had them for breakfast with honey and cream. A new and exciting experience and one anticipated for many long months! Now every few days we gather more. And we are discovering these same small native figs in the markets everywhere. It is a great year for figs and every few days we bring home another basket. Friends with fig trees invite us to come and pick. Side by side in the freezer with the peaches the figs begin to settle. I am told you can freeze them without even washing them.

"Cut off the stems and slip them into plastic bags. That's all you have to do," said a neighbor who has a great number of trees and shared a whole pailful with us.

Never in my wildest imaginings would I have believed we'd be growing a fig tree! There s something exotic and Biblical about growing figs. My name should be Rachel or Ruth, maybe, and I should be living in the middle of the Old Testament! I know the fig tree is symbolic. The last to leaf out in the spring, one thing it tells us perhaps is that when you're about to give up on anything—don't! Keep holding on and eventually something will loosen and move. In itself, the fig is a beautiful bush with three-lobed rich green leaves. What Bob first set out was five bare stalks, each about a yard high, and with a flourishing root. Having dug and fertilized the ground thoroughly, he carefully planted the stalks, firming the soil around them. After soaking them with the hose we noticed, lying on the ground nearby, a queer knob of root, shaped somewhat like a boomerang. We doubted it would thrive, but we casually shoved it under the red earth a little way off and then forgot about it. As spring advanced, we looked every few days for buds on the main plant. All the leaves on neighboring trees and shrubs were out before the figs even stirred. But eventually they came to life and so, incredibly, did the cast-off knob of root.

"Well," said Bob, as we watched those first leaves unfold and grow quite large, "we can never say we haven't a thing to wear!"

Actually, Adam was quite modest. With our ample rainfall of sixty inches a year all leaves in Tryon are enormous. I've seen tulip tree leaves large enough to sit on!

We all have friends for each season—seasons of feelings and interests. Some we laugh with, some we walk with, some we shop with, some we explore inner depths with. How fortunate I am to have a friend for all seasons. We enjoy everything together. In mutual trust we both are able to explore, and creatively, the depths of our feelings, our loves, our ideas, and even our fears. Our friendship is woven from deep affection and understanding and is of such a sturdy fabric that we never judge each other, never criticize. I feel completely accepted by her as I am, and I completely accept her as she is.

I believe we are drawn to certain people who become our friends because each has some particular trait that we ourselves also possess, but which, in us, lies dormant. The friend expresses it. Thus, unconsciously, we are drawn to him or her. In my experience this is consistently true. It may not be just one trait but many. How frequently this is evident in marriages. We say opposites attract, but isn't the characteristic, apparently missing in one, really there but out of sight? And maybe longing to emerge, and thus we are happy in the company of the one who is revealing it.

This particular friend of mine has such spontaneity, such freedom of expression. I feel, but am not always able to express to the degree that I feel. My friend delights me. It seems easy for her to be what she is and do what she feels. How many good and meaningful conversations we have together.

One afternoon she and I were sipping lemonade on the terrace and our discussion wandered into the realm of relationships. This priceless bit of wisdom came from my friend.

"Lately I've been thinking, Jean, if you meet people where they are you move for the moment away from where you are," she said. "You travel to a new and different area of being. In moving lies growth, growth and fresh experience, don't you think?"

"That's an interesting concept," I said, "and to me a new one."

"It seems to me," she went on, "if we stay in the spot where we are in a relationship, and do not move to meet the other person, we become static. We do not change, we do not grow, we miss the excitement and adventure of becoming for a time and maybe lastingly, something new and a little different. I say a little because you know we never can completely lose what is basically us nor do we want to."

We went on to discuss how every individual is unique, and my friend presented another fascinating idea.

"We expect water to be wet and a rock to be hard and accept them as they are. We don't try to make a rock into a cushion nor stand out in the rain and expect to be dry."

I guess we need to anticipate people being as they are and let them be thus. We need to accept the whole package complete.

When people do things that seem out of line can we take it as part of their pattern of the moment and accept?

Can we also accept the destructive and negative words of another as telling us more about where this person is at the moment than about his basic beliefs and character?

If I fail here I am judging.

The judgments we make, like the opinions we hold, affect us and, if negative, can wear down our arteries and nerves, and send the blood pressure soaring.

"What about individual opinions?" my friend asked. "It seems to me useful," I said, "and quite in order once in a while to slip into neutral. Surely we don't always have to have opinions about everything. It is good if we can listen and be quietly open to receive and learn. I don't believe it is *always* necessary nor even a good idea to express what we think."

Our sharing discussion wandered on to personal experiences of taking in stride the different inevitables. We were comparing the various ways we each had coped, and were coping—sometimes successfully and sometimes not. But always hoping to work around and through, to rise above and beyond the problem, be it physical or whatever.

Accepting the inevitable if we don't resist and resent can also bring about change in us, change that can be good. We will save a lot of energy by acting instead of reacting. Both acting and reacting consume energy. Acting takes you somewhere whereas reacting merely whips up your blood pressure. Acting also stirs and develops confidence in yourself.

I was looking at one of the most enchanting bouquets I had ever put together. I say "put together" because I'm not a flower arranger. I just pick blossoms and set them in a vase in a way that pleases me and perhaps breaks all rules. In my book flowers in vases don't have rules—they just please. This bouquet was composed of daisies, fragrant heads of lavender clover and some lovely wild yellow orchids. Countless small fringed florets clustered up a slim stalk, dainty and delicate and faintly scented. We'd gathered them along a mountain road an hour before. And now they stood on a table in our tent-trailer, for we were camping. A few days ago we set forth with Cloud Nine and settled ourselves beside a wildly rushing river in the Blue Ridge mountains, a little more than two hours from home.

Campers are so friendly. A very pleasant couple in the next site gave us salt when I found it was the one thing I had forgotten. As we got talking they invited us to visit them in Winter Park, Florida.

"Oh, by the way," the man said, as we turned to go back to our trailer, "what is your name?"

As we lit our nightly campfire the river tumbled at our backs, rushing over rocks and ledges. The music of the water kept us from hearing neighboring campers. Each day we walked and drove about exploring the mountains. We cooked and ate meals under the trees, sharing crumbs with the birds. Lovely deep-orange fungi emerged from very bright green moss bordering the river. Daily these grew, and more and more appeared all through the surrounding woods. Each one started out as a tiny button and ended up large as a saucer.

Back in Tryon the workmen were due to start building a guestroom. We had planned to camp for the first week, knowing that knocking out the house wall would be noisy. Besides, we were about ready for exploring the mountains in Cloud Nine. So here we were, enjoying the cooler air and the rather primitive surroundings. One afternoon we discovered a lookout off the Blue Ridge Parkway. With our recorders, we settled here to make music in a cool shaded spot with a view of range after range as far as we could see. Other vacationers, pausing to enjoy the vista, climbed down the mountainside to where we were playing. We were reminded again of how different people are. Some approached, clutching children by the hand fearful lest the youngsters walk on the wall and tumble over. Others came jauntily along, following children who had run freely ahead.

"What a wonderful way to spend your time," said one pleasant, out-going elderly woman traveling alone. We were playing "Greensleeves" at the time. "It sounds lovely," she added cheerily, as she climbed up the stone steps and out of sight. She was followed by another woman, clutching a large handbag. This one looked nervously at the view, standing well back from the edge. After glancing shyly at us and saying never a word, she turned and walked away.

Next, a gay young couple with several teenagers appeared. They paused and we talked a bit.

"We couldn't decide whether to come down," said the friendly young man, "but then we heard music and were so curious we had to come."

Another silent couple came, making no comment, thoroughly occupied in photographing the view and each other. Thinking how painful we must sound to anyone really musical I said, "I do hope you are not a symphony conductor!"

"Heavens, no," said the man. But he made no further comment and left us extremely curious as to what he did do. After we'd played a while we packed up our music and drove up the Parkway to a small mineral museum. Here we lost ourselves in gazing at cases of gem stones —garnets, sapphires, topaz, aquamarines, moonstones, amethysts, emeralds—all mined from the area. Another feature of great interest was a case of Kaolin and Hallosite. The latter, we learned, is used in china to give it a glossy whiteness. As to Kaolin, it seems that Josiah Wedgwood, in 1768, took five wagonloads of this from North Carolina to England to make the first Wedgwood china. I had no idea of the value and usability of all these minerals here. In the future I shall view china with even greater interest and respect, knowing that its ingredients may have been taken from the earth of our North Carolina mountains.

We had a lovely week, exploring brand new woods trails, discovering flowers new to us, falls hidden in the forest, reached by following their sound. One morning we lingered by a little woodland pond watching a family of ducks play in the water. First they were all gliding along the surface, shedding small Vs behind them. Next they were upended, seeking tidbits from the shallow bottom.

On our last day we located a motel clinging to the brink of a mountainside, with a never-ending view and a long balcony in front of all the rooms.

"We could come back in October," I said, "for a night or two and see the foliage. It will be fabulous here then."

"Let's do just that," Bob agreed.

After our week in the high Blue Ridge mountains we could scarcely wait to get home to see the progress in the Sunrise Room. We were amazed at all that had been accomplished since our departure—glass doors and windows in, partitions up.

To keep a steadying balance in life I like best to dwell in areas alternating between singing and yearning. When singing I'm usually in the now, with it, and thoroughly participating and feeling the moment. When singing I'm appreciating where I am, the scene around me, the reddening sourwoods across the street, the newly formed scarlet dogwood berries, our bright orange marigolds and white petunias along the garden path, the pattern of leaves against blue sky overhead.

It might be the lemon soufflé that rose up and up and broke open across the top to reveal a froth of gold; or the charming little wood mouse with a felt tail that plays in the woodpile. Or it may be the new library book that we are reading aloud at bedtime.

I'm singing as I gather tomatoes and pick crisp lettuce from the tiny salad garden for dinner; as I watch the sprinkler shedding rainbows over the garden along with sprays of water. I'm singing when I'm following an off-beat urge, doing something fun and purposeless and maybe a little bit crazy.

Today I'm singing because later we are going to drive out through Dark Corners, that erstwhile moonshine haven, to a little lonely lake surrounded by bushes and marsh grass. We will probably lie on the weathered gray wooden dock there, listening to the water lap the shore and watching the sun slide down behind the mountains.

Singing keeps joy in my heart—keeps my spirit soaring, ready to float on each new breeze.

Yearning is in its way just as important. I see yearning as a creative kind of restlessness that tells you something new is waiting, an untried path, an open door into a fresh new world. Yearning is a kind of reaching. Robert Browning has written: "Ah, but a man's reach should exceed his grasp or what's a heaven for?"

When a restlessness settles in on me it is usually because there is a little healthy longing deep down and I haven't recognized it. Yearnings can be gentle or sharp: they are life's nudges, prickings and pushes, that keep us from settling in a puddle and staying there. Some longings take weeks or months to float to the visible surface. Other times they may come in a whish. The quicker I can follow these with action the more satisfying. A little yearning holds us close to our instincts.

Yearning and singing together keep an even keel. A little too much of one or the other can stir a queer sort of discontent, an unexplainable heaviness. Whereas a little of each provides us with a milieu for balance in which to thrive and function at our best.

A good friend of mine recently wrote me this in a letter.

"Glimpses into eternal joys, fleeting as they may be, and peak experiences multiply their original effect if we make them the opportunity to express to others the joy and inspiration we feel. Then I'll be more because in addition to the original experience I'll be there to catch the reflection!"

We've a friend who used to be a decorator. One day I asked her to come over and see how we were getting along with the Sunrise Room and give us some color ideas. She came with armfuls of wallpaper, rug samples, and rug remnants from their house. Our builder and painter also brought masses of wallpaper books. We were snowed under. For days we pored through the sample books, and pondered, and finally came up with a luscious shade of yellow for the wall. We found some wallpaper for the stairwell and ceiling with a print of green growing bamboo on a white background.

When we go downstairs into the Sunrise Room we shall thus step into a pleached walk of green bamboo leading into a yellow room. I'm remembering the pleached walk in the Queen's garden at Kensington in London. It all becomes more intriguing every day, and we wish our son could watch his brainchild come into being.

It was a clear cool evening, the first one in a long hot week.

"Let's put the top down and drive up the mountain into the fresh night air and look at stars," Bob said.

A small sliver of moon hung over Hogback Mountain. Up and up we climbed, seeing more of the blue-black heavens and stars with each curve. The stars were bright and large, spilling through the clear dark sky. Here was the Milky Way, and the Dippers large and small, Cassiopeia, the Pleiades, and Delphinus. We were each pointing out our favorites and reminding one another. And now we saw, up near the mountain tops and along the road ahead, a number of pinpricks of light—not quite stars. Or were they? Stars? Houselights? Stars that had strayed to earth, held prisoner there? Houselights that wandered up to heaven? Who knows? Rounding a bend all these points of light seemed to mingle, both reaching up into the night sky and tumbling down the mountain slopes. How could we tell where earth ended and heaven began? Do we need to?

Along the roadsides golden rod and Joe Pye weed emerge; we bring home armfuls to stand in the tall bamboo vase outside the front door. Everywhere through the meadows sweeps a tumbled foam of late yellow tickseed sunflowers. Things are happening—there is a subtle turn in the season. The sourwood foliage is bronzing and in some places has become dark red. Here and there a stray bough of maple has turned scarlet. Dogwoods have ripened their bright red berries close on the same branch with next year's buds. But still we swim every day and cozy in with our air conditioning during the noon heat.

Out in the garden marigolds are brilliant and numerous. The last figs keep on ripening, each day a few more. Tomatoes are ten feet tall and growing higher, beanstalk fashion. We picked four red ones and two yellows this morning. How fragrant they are in your hand when just off the vine.

The jack-in-the-pulpit seed heads of tight berries are a brilliant red. Nature's way is to let the stem rot so the heavy seed clusters fall to the rich pine-needle-covered earth, where they can settle in and send down roots and grow if let alone. Acorns tumble onto the brick terrace, each with a plop. What if one landed on our heads, I wonder, as I weed along the garden path. It would hurt, I guess. The Oregon grape has small seedling children six or eight inches tall near the parents. The ajuga is ready for more thinning. This means we will have another bushel to plant outside the Sunrise Room and along the path going down. The crabapple tree swings gay little orange apples on its branches. The changes of the turning season blow on the breeze, and breathe through the sunlight.

As always at summer's end something in us clings, and something more vital draws forward, eager to meet the newness and fresh directions, the excitements and joys fall and winter will bring.

Last night we saw a lunar moth. It was fluttering around the garden light, its pale-green frosted wings catching and reflecting the glow. We went outside to watch. It darted here and there, now up to the light, now down to the holly bush beneath. Finally it lit on the screen and for a few moments its whole body and wings vibrated. Then it grew still.

Even in the beam of our flashlight it never moved. What a scrap of wonder, what a gloriously lovely creature—with feathery feelers, soft fragile wings, translucent, and as if powdered with light-green mist. Small eye-spots decorated the wings, and the hind pair each had a long sweeping tail. Is any creature in nature lovelier? Surely, while admiring this beautiful moth we can think of none.

Would our moth be there in the morning? No, it was gone. A creature of the night only who, according to Palmer's *Natural History*, hangs by day hidden out of sight under the leaves with wings folded. This enlightening tome also tells us that the lunar moth has no economic value! These magnificent creatures of the evening then have no useful material purpose in the scheme of things? They just *are*. To me this makes them even more fascinating.

We had stood looking long at that lunar moth. Look and study and give over to any one thing and something happens to you—something opens you to new awarenesses. You enter a world undefined. Be it a flower, a leaf, a beetle or a great cloud in the heavens, we are someway a little different afterward. It is as if something of what we are studying enters deeply into us, bringing more than we outwardly see.

Nights at this season we have a small owl that who-o-o-os. This enchanting little fluttery sound ripples through the blackness. Who-o-o-o—? Eternal question. Who is who—who is there—who am I—Who are you—Who-o-o-o? Like life, on and on with questions but never answers. But now for the little screech owl there is an answer from somewhere way off. At first faint, but growing louder, comes the responding whoo-o-o, then the two are who-ing back and forth. In the world of owls I'm sure that who-o-o-o is much more than an unanswered question!

Although these are the little Eastern screech owls, their calls are more tremulous and gentle than the name implies. The book says they weigh about six ounces. They hatch downy-white. Wouldn't I love to see a tiny one, fresh out of the egg, just dried off and fluffy! Amazingly, they have a temperature of a hundred and one! I was concerned until I found that the great horned owl and the barn owl have temperatures of a hundred and five and a hundred and three respectively. While hot little creatures all three, our owl is the coolest.

The Eastern screech owl carries a heavy burden of superstition. Its quavering call is claimed to be prophetic and to foretell calamity, disease and death. But opposed to this ominous foreboding is a cheerful note. You may protect yourself, when you hear this owl in the night, if you rise from bed and turn your left shoe upside-down. This simple act saves you from disaster. However, if you live in Mississippi calamity may still be breathing down your neck unless you also turn your left trouser pocket inside-out. Here a shoe alone won't do. There is quite a bit of documented evidence, they say, proving that if you do these things, evil is safely averted! So you may listen to this little being of the dark happily, knowing that his plaintive note, actually a love call, will do you no harm.

Along with the sound of the owl we hear the distant train whistle, also a lonesome and nostalgic sound. The two merge into a never-ending quest in which we are all engaged.

Are answers important? Maybe not. I'm not happy with too many ready-made and complete answers. One overall answer I can accept and like, though, is that *being* is more important than questing: the here and now is more alive than the "where from," "why" and "where to." Man is born with innate curiosity so he will always speculate. But after briefly wondering I prefer to forget questions and tune in to the lunar moths and the small owls in our lives. They waken us to a sense of the magnitude and mystery in nature. And to an awareness of God back of it all, our common dwelling place. It is then the earth speaks to us, it is then the earth reaches through to touch us. The touch of the earth, drawn from vastness, sifts through into each individual, only to reach out again to shape the larger pattern, the pattern that includes everything from the flower at my feet to the farthest star.

9

September Is Change

SEPTEMBER is change—the pause between summer and fall—cool days with mountains sharp and clear, an ivory sky at dawn and sunset.

Days still can be very warm. We swim, we walk, we garden, we wear summer clothes, and yet there is a hint of change in the air. A slight sadness comes over me as I look at the wild iris tired from the summer, and brown at the edges. The climbing roses on the fence have tossed aside all foliage, but now and again lazily send forth a red flower on a bare stalk. Bunches of jack-in-the-pulpit seeds lying on the pine needles are scarlet.

Over at the Inn where we swim, the mimosa trees around the pool are covered with green pods filled with little green bumps of seed. They remind me of the sugar-pod peas that you eat, pods and all. One day recently, drifting in the blue water of the pool, I kept looking up at these pods overhead and wondering what they would taste like cooked. Someone has to be the first. Think what courage it took to try the first lobster! But I guess I am not that experimental. Presently my attention was directed and held by the magic of interlacing circles of shimmering sunlight and rainbows on the pool bottom.

Everywhere in our vicinity a few leaves in the woods have turned red or maroon, here and there a whole branch of scarlet foliage stands out. The sourwood trees are especially beautiful now, creamy fringed tassels swing from topmost branches. The foliage is bronzing up too. Night insects of midsummer are still with us but are slowing down slightly. They sing, but less and less through the month.

Certain birds are still singing in the morning before light. The perky little brown Carolina wren is one we can always count on. The nuthatch and the tufted titmouse, pine siskins and the cardinal are delightfully invading the garden, reminding us that soon we must get the feeder out and lay in a supply of sunflower seeds. These days from off through the woods comes the occasional harsh call of the pileated woodpecker. Does he, too, remember that he enjoyed our suet last year?

While we are loosing and letting go of one season, we are also welcoming the next. I'll have to admit that sometimes it's with a little tug that I loose and let go of any special period of living, or any season that has been a particularly rich one. With the delicious impersonality of nature the present month will slip away and the next one come regardless of me. Alas, I do tend to cling to joys that were. It is all right, I tell myself, to relive and draw strength from the good that has been, but holding on is something else again. How can I have room to embrace the next good that comes our way if I am cluttered up clutching that which has gone before? I know this but all the same I am holding a little to this lovely past season. There is, I find, an interesting gap between the knowing something we should do, or think, or feel, and making it a part of us and really doing it.

This summer has been a very fine one with the garden so perfect, visiting friends, books we have read, and of course the local peaches and dazzling crepe myrtle!

I always like the freedom of summer, the outdoor season. Picnics, informal meals, many eaten outdoors. In Tryon we can picnic and eat out almost all year, and garden too, for that matter. But then, summer is the special time for these activities. While our winters are mild, we do have a rare inch or more of snow. But it's usually gone by noon. Except of course for the famous time a few years ago that people love to tell of, the seventeen-inch blizzard. On the day Norme was set for an operation in the hospital, he and Betty woke to all those inches of white.

"Well," said Norme, buckling on his snowshoes, "I'd better leave plenty of time, can't tell how many drifts there are."

So he set forth, snowshoeing, his essentials in a pack on his back, and had his operation on schedule. After a few paralyzing days, because Tryon is not used to this kind of weather, the snow melted and disappeared. And Norme came home by car, not realizing he had created a legend. However, we're not thinking about snow these warm September days, but about the imminent chrysanthemum buds, and the blossoms on the camellias, the fall-flowering sasanquas, which will be out any moment.

Bob has gone up to Cape Cod for a week to visit Kay and Del, his sister and brother-in-law. I am alone. I have a self that loves to be alone and a self that needs companionship. All week first one was in the ascendency, then the other. As soon as Bob goes out of town I go immediately to the library for a stack of books and then line up a few projects on the place to do to surprise him. This time I was starting and enjoying *Bring me a Unicorn* by Anne Lindbergh, and getting after some cupboards and drawers and re-demothing the clothes bags. This is the week I plan to have different friends in for lunch, and I will not miss a day in the Mimosa Inn swimming pool!

We've had no rain for over a week and every day warm sun. The ground is dry. All of us gardeners are watering. Watering is pure delight here in Tryon because we have discovered the most intriguing sprinkler imaginable.

Basically a long bar with holes in it, it sends up beautiful flaring streams of water that scatter broadly as they thoroughly soak a very large area. The sprinkler is in constant motion. A kind of mobile, actually, as it swings from one side to the other in a slow and leisurely arc. The arc is large and we leave the sprinkler on for two or three hours in one place. It takes only one move and two positions to do our entire garden. No more constantly shifting about of small, whirling sprinklers. The appealing qualities of this one are revealed when you sit and watch it, especially in the late afternoon sunshine when, fringing the spray, small rainbows dart hither and yon. You never can be quite sure where they will flutter next.

I had just finished watering today when the rain came. The sky above the mountains turned a deep blue-black. There was complete stillness in the woods, followed by a faint rumble of thunder up toward Saluda.

Then it came, the first large drops scattering dark red discs over the brick terrace. There is nothing, but nothing, like the fragrance of the first few moments of rain after a dry week. All the life and vitality of the earth emerges in that scent. I always have to step out and breathe it in and revel. Twice I revel. First, because of the aroma and, secondly, because the garden is getting much needed water. In a few minutes it was pouring; the rain driving horizontally through the woods and beating loudly on the roof. I stood on the balcony watching.

Tryon has its gentle rains, but this was not one of them. This one was violent as it brushed in silver gusts through the trees. The wind was wild and the trees bent to it. Clouds of rain swept through branches, loosing one here or a leaf cluster there. I was caught on the balcony in a kind of spell, watching the dance of the trees. How flexible they were, bending almost to a right angle and weaving back and forth together. Would any snap off? There is that great leaning pine, leaning, fortunately, away from the house. Could this take one more storm? It swayed madly with its neighbors but held firm.

How alive a storm is, I thought, as

beyond the screen small branches flew past me. All the forces of nature were gathered there in this blow. Watching, I wondered if I would be afraid, but I was more exhilarated. I guess we cannot feel two emotions at once, both fear and excitement. In me, fear gave way to the drama of the moment. The strength of the storm was magnificent and stirring. I began to sense that behind the visible blow and rain and tossing trees was the whole vast power of nature herself. This storm was just a small bit of force let out, a front for an infinite power somewhere beyond.

How magnificent to witness nature in this mood. My inner forces stirred and wakened, wanting to rise up and merge with those energies loosed there in the woods.

At one point I was struggling to close the balcony doors into the bedroom while the water was pouring in. Bob would do this so easily. For me they were ornery. While I stood pushing them closed I could feel the strength of the storm against me.

Nature's moods are varied and all of them waken some response in us, whether we are conscious of it or not. What a contrast was the quiet stillness of yesterday's golden early morning, last night's star-spangled heavens, and a recent breath-holding dusk when the thrush was singing in the sourwood down by the brook. Dusk, it seems to me, is nature holding her breath. The "in" breath, the time of activity, is the day; the "out" breath, the letting go and relaxing, is the night. Dusk is the pause between.

Mountain storms soon pass, and within the hour the sun was shining. The rain gauge showed one and three-quarters inches in that half hour: The terrace ran with streams. The paved road was shiny black and small active rivers gushed along the gutters. The geraniums were blown over and some of the blossom stalks broken. Oddly enough the one thing that seemed to weather everything was the maidenhair fern. Perhaps because it does not stand stiffly resisting showers and storms like the geraniums but bends with every breeze. Fresh and green, live and vital it stands now, yet appearing so delicate. Like some people I know, it has hidden strength and vitality, far more than you can ever know or see.

After the storm a delicious stillness is over all outdoors. The mood of force of a few hours back has given way to another quiet one. Everywhere in the woods a steaming mist floats and rises among the trees while wet leaves gleam in the sunlight, countless shining threads of light.

Carl and Gladys took me to the Tea House on Lake Lanier for Sunday dinner. So thoughtful when Bob is away.

The terrace over which spreads a huge liquid amber tree is covered with small tables and umbrellas in gay colors. Inside, you select from a buffet of fabulously delicious food, and outside you settle and eat. All the while small boats dart and swish over the blue waters towing people water-skiing. The backdrop of Lake Lanier is a line of mountains, Hogback, Rocky Spur and Melrose. All towering serenely above on this fresh, sunny September day.

A marvelous dinner, chicken with some kind of herbs. Also sweet potato pone, like an ambrosial soufflé, light, airy and sweet. For dessert, meringues with chocolate sauce. So interesting to watch the motor boats weaving over the lake, each one sending receding blue furrows behind. We were too far off to be disturbed by the noise but near enough to feel a part of the motion and rhythm.

Relaxing there with good friends, surrounded by other diners, some of whom were neighbors, eating marvelous food, speaking of this and that, and with soft music in the offing, created in us three a mood of contentment and peace. Each separate group of people there on the terrace was in their own world. Yet we all, in occasionally exchanging smiles and a few words, were drawn close and at one in the sharing in and merging with the surrounding beauty. Happiness lies in small things!

Bob has been away five days now and I am lonesome. But I am glad he has gone because it is good to have him enfolded in family, nieces, nephews and cousins, and his sister and her husband. Also it is actually a part of our life-style at times to separate for a few days or a week and go different directions.

How much we each bring back to the other from these independent excursions, and what a true joy it is when we get together after one. As the Indian poet Kahlil Gibran writes:

> . . . But let there be spaces in your togetherness,
> And let winds of heaven dance between you . . .
> Fill each other's cup but drink not from the one cup . . .
> Sing and dance together and be joyous, but let each of you be alone
> Even as the strings of the lute are alone though they quiver with the same music . . .
> And stand together yet not too near together:
> For the pillars of the temple stand apart,
> And the oak tree and the cypress grow not in each other's shadow.

Two more days and Bob will be home. Meanwhile I decided to telephone him tonight. A lovely thought to hold through the day. How wonderful his voice sounded, warm and responsive. They were watching the sun set over the bay. We exchanged doings these last days since we had been separated, and I hung up with a comfortable happy feeling. I got into bed with my book, and soon drifted off, purely content to have had that contact over a thousand land miles.

When I get impatient with some of the things civilization brings, like crowded cities, pollution, drugs and such, I have to pause and remember the telephone that bridges distances and brings families and friends close.

Bob was home. I met the plane at dusk and we had supper on the porch by candlelight.

We were standing looking down at the reflections in our pond. We could see the moon gently nudged by a ruffle of cloud and, mirrored in the black water, a single branch tangling with both cloud and moon. Our pond is a pond by special courtesy as it is about twenty inches by fifteen. But it is exactly the right size for our small Japanese garden. If by night it reflects the moon and a few stars, and if in the daylight a patch of blue sky and a hint of oak leaves, what more could we want? Tiny perky-tailed cocoa-brown wrens come to bathe here, and a pair of dignified cardinals. And sometimes tufted titmice and all sorts of small charming Southern birds, pine siskins, cedar waxwings, and others whose names we are gradually learning.

This particular night seemed one of special beauty and enchantment because of the week apart. Our glow surely must have beamed from us to mingle with the shine of the moon on the water. Everywhere were the dancing shadow patterns of the shrubs against the picket fence that encloses the area. Gardenias, camellias, Oregon grape, box, and holly border the garden path, and toward one end the gray stone Japanese lantern gently lifts the four corners of its tilted stone roof, tilted to coast any lurking evil spirits up and away!

We walked together along the garden path, appreciating our surroundings, the moon and a few stars, each other, everything, including our house and garden here in the foothills of the Blue Ridge. We had much news to exchange. Though but a family of two these days, with our three children married and living elsewhere, it is very nice when we are complete.

This morning in rather a hazy just-awake state I looked out the bathroom window to be startled by the dazzling scarlet of lycoris radiata. A single airy-fairy blossom cluster on a slender stalk had emerged from the red-orange soil. This is the most astonishing flower and almost impossible to describe. Suddenly in September it appears out of the earth. First a slim stem with a cluster of graceful tapering buds at the tip that you hardly notice. This is followed by feathery red flowers. The petals are delicate as tissue paper and countless anthers from the flower centers swing upward at the outer edges until the bloom seems about to float off. After the blossom passes, foliage like daffodil greenery emerges and lasts until spring. When the greenery dies down you forget all about lycoris until that surprising day the following September when you again are startled by an arresting bloom.

These are the days of silver spiderwebs, wherever you look or walk. Gardening or wandering about I am forever tangling in them. I'm sorry about this because each one is a work of art. I don't like to keep disrupting the private life of the spider. But

I don't always see them until I feel the threads of web in my hair, or across my arm. Then it's too late. I trust spiders are patient and don't mind rebuilding. They must be, the way they sit for hours waiting for a meal to come along. Every web seems to have three or four threads to make it fast, and these can be quite long. It is these that I'm forever getting caught up in because I always watch out for the spiders themselves. How beautiful are the webs each morning after a night rain or heavy dew when spangled with silver drops, and you see so clearly the intricate patterns. One wise spider has built right by the outside light. Each night its webs are filled with food for a week! But what about the less intelligent one who began to build in my clothes closet with never an insect to pass by? I caught him in a glass, took him out, and loosed him in the garden.

In addition to spiders, we have lizards with little blue tails. I really love these little creatures and enjoy watching them dozing in the sun or skittering through the leaves.

Next to lizards daddy-long-legs are my favorites of the smaller wild life, and they are very much in evidence this time of year.

They love the porch ceiling outside the front door. Here they gather and we see them conducting nightly revels around the front door frame. But today I really communicated with one. Bob and I were eating early supper on the terrace— meatloaf sandwiches and melon and pink mint tea. All at once along the bench toward my tray there came swinging a daddy-long-legs, his walk almost a dance. He looked at me and I looked at him. His small round body is a golden tan, but the wonder of his legs and how he maneuvers them is a true miracle. Seven legs he had. I looked him up in palmer's *Natural History*, and he should have eight. I thought they seemed unevenly spaced. But he managed very well. Sometimes we humans have enough trouble managing two legs— just imagine having eight and, proportionately, that long! The book also says these intriguing creatures have no economic value. This makes them even more appealing. I do like things that just purely *are* and have no purpose. Daddy-long-legs, I read, stand pointing in the direction cows are to be found. But actually they point in all directions. Of course, I suppose if you go far enough in any direction you are bound to meet a cow. In any case it's an interesting bit of lore.

My little friend here had an interesting way of bending his knees to let his body sink lower, to touch what was beneath him. When he was going somewhere he first raised himself up. As he moved around near me for a while he seemed quite free of fear, and then all at once he became attracted by my sandwich, so I gave him a breadcrumb. Imagine attacking a mound of food larger than your body (in his case not counting legs.) But undaunted, he did, and seemed to enjoy it. For moments he ate off one side, making no impression at all on the crumb. What would it be like to be as small as my little friend here? How differently the world must appear through the eyes of a daddy-long-legs. I love to watch them move about. Those ridiculous legs like fine hairs are beautifully made with wonderfully flexible joints where needed. He has some almost invisible little feelers around the front of his body too. He seemed to stroke the breadcrumb with these as he ate.

Thank goodness the little lizards that we

missed all the first part of the summer are coming back. They are so scary and skitter off fast when you make even a slight movement, let alone try to come near them. Their scarcity this year, I suspect, is due to the chlordane we put on the garden to combat moles and pine mice. These underground creatures ate many of our bulbs last spring. But still, I'm sure we never should have used chlordane. Not only did it give my organic-gardening soul a twinge, but I fear it reduced the lizard population. It was midsummer before we saw the first one.

Gardeners have such a ridiculous built-in sense of hope, faith, and recklessness. In spite of losing to mice and moles over one hundred crocuses and countless other bulbs, Bob and I are now wondering how many we should plant this year. Wayside Gardens, with the sheer beauty of their annual catalogue, aid and abet this hope and faith and recklessness. We marvel as we pore through their pages and catch ourselves traveling off in all sorts of new directions. Why not order ranunculus? Never grew it before, but why not?

Last night we had dinner with Betty and Norme on their terrace and watched dusk turn to night and the first stars prick through the heavens—and then the moon rose. Later, heading home, Bob suggested that we drive up the Hogback road and watch the moon over the mountains.

It was full, and we had the top down. How brilliant were the peaks and valleys, and everywhere the white moonlight streamed and shimmered. We drove up to where the pavement ends and on beyond to a favorite spot where we often go. Here the mountains fade off into the distance, away to infinity, layer on layer. A few rugged trees in the foreground at the road edge give a sense of perspective. These are the ranges of the Blue Ridge that we look off at, silver veils drawn gently across the horizon, too beautiful for words. We sat in silence, feeling a part of the scene and the wonder before us.

How different are mountains in various parts of the world. The Alps of Switzerland have a majesty and vigor, a drama and a dazzling splendor that stirs and stimulates. But here in Tryon the mountains are different. They are intimate and close by.

You almost feel you can reach out and touch them. They are gentle mountains, their contours soft and quietly rolling. There is majesty and grandeur here, too, but of a different sort. Be it Switzerland or Tryon, we happen to like mountains. There is a foreverness about them, an endurance. Their original folding up out of the new-made earth is thought-provoking and a marvel to contemplate. Did they come all at once, bursting suddenly out of the cosmos when the earth was new? Or did they emerge gradually, through aeons? Geogologists would have this answer in complex scientific terms, but I don't really want the information. I prefer to dream my own dreams about their beginnings.

I never tire of looking at mountains. That night, cozy in our car there on the rim of the world, our minds began wandering down delicious byways of the past to wonder about the first people who lived in this area, in these valleys, and on the mountain meadows, on the peaks, in the coves, by the waterfalls, and along the wild rhododendron- and laurel-bordered streams. Who were they and what were they like? A hardy group they must have been with ways quite different from ours.

Happily sitting there on the top of things, we recalled one of our favorite stories of the region—the romance of Miss Emma and Jim Fetty. Jim Fetty was a lone mountain man who had lost two wives, and he was eyeing with favor the widow Miss Emma who came gaily down the path past his house on her way to market each week. This particular day Jim was sitting on his stoop, wriggling his bare toes contentedly in a puddle of sun-warmed muddy water, and looking smugly off toward the field where he had a good bit of saved-up money buried.

Miss Emma came swinging along in her crisp blouse and full skirt, looking mighty appealing to this lone widower whose kitchen was piled high in dirty dishes, and whose pants shore needed mending. She had a sweet gentleness about her that had been gradually winning Jim for some weeks now.

So when she stopped to chat a little he felt the strangest stirring inside himself, and she across the fence, so runs the tale, was feeling equally fluttery.

After a few casual exchanges, Miss Emma said, "That porch shore is a sight."

"Ah, maybe so, but a man don't know how to do by his lone," Jim replied.

"Happen someday I'll jest slip down and red things up for you if you'd like," she replied with a smile, amazed to hear herself speak up so quickly.

Her quiet voice, her sweet face and engaging smile pushed him along far faster than he intended.

"Miss Emma," he said, suddenly standing up, "you see this here peg on the porch wall with a hoe on it? That there's my first woman's hoe, and on that next peg hangs my second woman's hoe." Pointing to the empty third peg, he said, "How'd you like to hang yourn thar?"

That was how it started, and before long there was a church wedding, the pants got mended, the porch got straightened, and the kitchen red up! And a hoe now hung on the third peg.

For a week now we have had perfect weather, clear and crisp and September in essence. And for ten days we've had no air conditioning. We do bless this modern convenience during the hot spells of July and August. Those soaring summer temperatures are the price we pay for warm January days when we eat in the sunshine on the terrace. On midsummer days we turn on the air conditioning, close all doors and windows, and that is that. But after it's dark we open up again and sleep with fresh mountain air. Now we are happy to have everything open and feel real live air, day *and* night. I always suspect that air that has been conditioned has lost something. After breathing it for a long while no matter how hot it is, I have to step outside for a few good whiffs of air that is un-tampered-with.

This morning I have been out in the garden pulling weeds. The strawberry plants are flowering. Will we have berries this fall?

Here are the chrysanthemum cuttings made early in the summer. Now they are beautiful potted plants with buds on them, such is this salubrious climate. Over by the gray stone Japanese lantern is a rhododendron bud, showing pink and about to bloom. Does it think it's spring? By the wall the perennial begonia is flourishing, covered with flowers and buds. The Aix-les-Bains geranium is flowering, two blossoms, airy and delicate, and a deep Valentine pink. They have a distinctly foreign and French air. These were also a present.

As I look about the garden, I realize how much in it was given us. Wherever my eye lights I am reminded of friend or neighbor. This is a good kind of garden. And now, after three years, we are happy to be able to share our surplus with others who are receptive.

I've experienced a good many romantic moments when engaged in what is usually considered a mundane occupation—that of hanging up the wash. This happens to be one of my favorite pastimes. A few days after Bob got home the morning was clear and sunny, just right for lines and laundry. I am convinced that there could be no more beautiful laundry-hanging spot than ours. It is just this side of the entrance to the woodland path that zigzags to the brook. The line stretches from tree to tree, going three ways and forming a triangle. You have to walk around gardenias, January jasmine, and those little stakes that tell us where we're going to put daffodils in another few weeks.

Pairs of socks look trim and neat hung up in rows. Napkins, white and gleaming, absorb and reflect back the sunlight. Bath towels, washcloths and sheets add their assortment of shapes, colors and textures. All phases of living are represented here on the line. Inside is a dryer which we welcome on rainy days or in winter! But not today when a small brown wren sings overhead, when somewhere in the distance a cardinal responds, and just there above me a squirrel chatters as he ruffles his tail. A nuthatch and a tufted titmouse are helping themselves to sunflower seeds from a great big head we have hanging from a branch. No, today I'm exactly where I want to be, where I belong and doing exactly what I want to do. The clothes are where they want to be too, absorbing the sunshine and fresh air that they will later give back to us. The scent of all outdoors clings to clothes which dry in the sunlight, and it emanates from them indoors.

This turned out to be one of those wonderful days when *all* we do right on through seems touched with glamour.

"Shall we frost the cake?" I said after supper. It was barely seven. We appreciate early suppers on the porch these late summer evenings. One of our retirement joys is dinner at noon and then a light night meal at six. What beautiful long evenings this gives us. Besides, I'm getting dinner in the morning when I'm full of early-in-the-day energy.

I found out that Homer's birthday is this week. He and John, who live across the street, are coming for dinner tomorrow, so I had made a golden angel cake.

"Let's go out on the terrace," Bob said, after the cake was frosted, "and have a concert." We sat there together, listening to records, beginning with Schumann's Symphony no. 2, conducted by Bernstein. We had heard this symphony at Philharmonic Hall in New York before we moved South and had loved it live. And we were liking it again here in the garden waiting for the first star.

We would each see our own first star. After a few moments mine came, tangled in the leaves of the Southern magnolia. Bob had to move to see it and I had to shift about to see his. His was over the dogwood and crepe myrtle. The sky behind both was deepening blue—a near-twilight tint. I guess no matter how close we are to another, we can see only our own star from where we sit. Of course, when we move over to where the other person is, we can see his star. But not if we stay glued to our own personal spot.

Music always sounds lovely outdoors. Gradually the heavens darken and more stars than we can count emerge, all in a tangle of treetops. Now we share dozens. But those first personal ones have special meaning. A star—a single star, and the first in all the vastness of the new night sky— can be something different for each of us —a personal response—a message—a direction—a wish—a dream.

10

The Touch of October

OCTOBER spreads through the mountains and valleys in constantly changing shadows of blue. When the sun sets, as if reluctant to leave such splendor, it reaches back across the heavens with long fingers of pale orange and smoky violet. October is crisp and cool around the edges with dazzling sun. Distances are clear and far.

"Mountains are like music, the great kind of music that is everything you have ever known about and something more," writes Alberta Pierson Hannum. To me they are Beethoven, vast and great, stretching our perceptions well beyond ourselves. They are Sibelius too, with cool green forests in his melodies, and Wagner, magnificent and thunderous. The little coves and streams, the waterfalls and valleys with corn growing and mules grazing in the sunlight are Mozart and

Haydn. In October our whole world is not only blue shadows and great music but a gradually rising crescendo of vibrant color.

About the middle of the month the green foliage begins to fade and give way while gradually, very gradually, warmer colors drift over the mountain shoulders. At first the change comes more as a translucence, a sense of light in the woods, with here and there a bright branch. But little by little appear the scarlets, pure deep golds, crimson, and the subtle violet of the maple leaf vibernum. The music and rhythm of brilliant color is reaching its real peak.

Meanwhile, every few days in the late afternoon, we drive up Melrose mountain to watch the changes. On the mountain approaching three thousand feet colors come sooner. We enjoy autumn wild flowers along the roadside, purple asters, goldenrod, blue ageratum, Joe Pye weed, wild phlox, and countless varieties of yellow daisies. I brought back an armful of flowers and they now stand in the tall bamboo vase outside the front door to greet all who come.

After dark the stars, vague and hidden by mists during the hot months, are bright and sparkling, and myriads stream across the heavens, while in its time the moon sends clear shadows over the brick terrace and the whole garden.

All of nature swings gently as the seasons softly, imperceptibly turn. Each month touches not only the countryside differently, the wild life, all gardens everywhere, but us. Though scarcely aware of it, we respond in countless ways to seasonal changes.

What is the touch of October?

October is the month of quickening, of new beginnings. Something fresh and exciting wakens and stirs within us during the cooler days and crisper nights. While the mountains that have been a dreamy blue summer haze suddenly sharpen and reveal themselves a vivid silhouette against the sky, we, too, feel our soft relaxed edges, compatible with lazy summer days, firm up into a more definite outline. Keen and alert, we are filled with plans for the fall ahead, new directions, new interests, while the shape of the winter before us begins to form and to cast a long shadow before it.

In the garden chrysanthemums are opening, mauve, tawny orange, yellow, deep red. The buds of the sasanqua camellias, pink-tipped, are gradually unfolding. The white ones with gold centers are coming too. You cannot stay indoors. Something about these dazzling days lures you out. This morning before breakfast, and before it was really quite light, I was setting out young chrysanthemum plants. Last June I trimmed the plants back to about one foot and potted up a good number of trimmings. With our ample summer rainfall these tips soon rooted and began to grow. We had summered them in a shady spot where they developed beautifully from June until now. Today the ground is damp, inviting me to plant. Each pot is a mass of roots, and I set them along outside the fence to fill in spaces in a large area of massed chrysanthemums. I also put a dozen inside the fence where we'll see them from the living room. Not only have all these cuttings become sturdy plants since June, but most of them are covered with buds.

Our rough cedar fence is six feet high, and encloses a brick terrace and a garden. The fence is made of two-inch uprights set a quarter of an inch apart with the necessary 4 x 4s to hold it up. Outside the fence runs the road up the mountain. Growing against it there are the chrysanthemums, naturalized daffodils, red climbing roses, pyracantha, and clematis. These are for the pleasure of the passersby. The space inside the fence is our very private domain. A woodsy garden path forms a half circle out from one end of the terrace and back at the other. It leads through pine-needle-covered earth set here and there with bushes and plants, mostly naturalized and no set flower beds. This is our garden, Japanese in feeling and colorful with vivid azaleas, myrtle, ajuga, holly, Oregon grapes, iris, and countless other shrubs and flowers, including plenty of local wild flowers. It is mainly a spring garden. In summer we enjoy the cool greenness, spiced with a few gay pink and red impatiens plants. At all seasons our large floor-to-ceiling living-room windows bring the garden indoors.

Two of our favorite outdoor features are the Japanese stone lantern and the small pool I have mentioned. Often when we spend the evening on the terace under the stars we light the candle in the lantern and watch flickering shapes and shadows slide over the ground. The bird bath we made, and it was simple. We scooped out the earth, spread cement in the hollow, then arranged interesting rocks around the rim, tucking bright green moss in the chinks. Our friend, an iron Japanese turtle, lifting his head to the sun, lives on one of these rocks. Though the stream at the bottom of the woodland is always running, we like having water even nearer by where we can step outdoors and watch a single waterbug coast over the surface, a cloud mirrored, or a bird bathing.

We are also very fond of our terrace table which is a large millstone. I enjoy studying the small furrows and often imagine how, in days of old, the grain worked its way along these. Our millstone transports me into a long-gone era. A visit to Cade's Cove in the Smokies and Cable's Mill there that operates today shows how they used to use these great round stones. Standing in that weathered wooden building, listening to the sound of the water from the turning wheel outside, you hear a crunching, grinding noise. You watch the kernels of corn go into a funnel at the top and trickle out through a little chute at the bottom where an elderly man sits and bags the fine white cornmeal. Visitors like us can then take some home to cook with.

I like to imagine our own particular millstone years back grinding corn in some secluded community in a remote mountain area. I can see, nearby, the brown family mule with long soft ears moving gently as he pulls up grass. And just over there fields of corn flourish, and maybe sorghum. Today in our garden this millstone is a table and through this last summer we have had half a dozen pink and white potted geraniums standing in the center. After languishing during the hot weeks, these are now burgeoning. Bob fed them 0-14-14 recently too, and I'm sure this started the burgeoning. Now that a frost could come any night they seem to be giving their all. They are not only covered with huge blossoms, but clusters of buds on charming little crook necks. The French geranium is also aglow with deep pink blossoms.

In the market this morning Mr. Cowan said, picking me out a cantaloupe for breakfast tomorow, "These are the best ones now coming in—and the last. That's the way it is," he added, nodding his head thoughtfully, "towards the end of their season everything is at its best—us too, maybe," he added with a twinkle.

Certainly all flowers seem to put forth their very greatest efforts before the frost. Our geraniums were never like this!

Yesterday Bob came home with a large bag of sunflower seeds and a great clump of suet. Last year he made a suet basket of hardware cloth and attached it to the trunk of the Spanish oak on the terrace. He set it just higher than the neighboring dogs can reach but not too high for us. Ten minutes after he put in the suet this morning there arrived a nuthatch coming down the tree upside down, head first. Why always head first? Does he like to see what is before him that he's aiming for? And now there is a woodpecker with a red spot on its head descending the trunk. But it backs down, right side up. Does it like to be surprised when it arrives? I guess we all have moods to match each bird. On occasion we like to see where we're heading and other times we prefer surprises.

Of course I'm planting my own human reactions on the mysteries of nature here, which I know is unscientific and illegal, but who wants to be scientific and legal always? We can never know why any creature follows any particular pattern. Nature is filled with provocative whys, and unanswered questions, and is ever coming up with more questions than answers. How often we pause in wonder before these inexplicables, and feel our respect stir for the immense power and forces among which we live and move. Our self-respect rides high too as we sense ourselves a part of this vast overall pattern.

What a comfortable and contented feeling to look at the small window garden in my study. Each day now I bring in another plant or two. A cheerful note of green they lend. I am especially enjoying the basil. We've been using it all summer, chopped up in the salad, snipped into the soup. Scrambled eggs or omelets with chopped basil have an exotic flavor. I also love it with buttered boiled potatoes, minced fine, along with, or in place of, parsley. Basil and cream cheese sandwiches are delicious. By summer's end the plants have grown tall and leggy in the garden. I have cut off the tops and set these in a glass of water to root, sharing my surplus trimmings with friends for them to do the same. My original three plants were given us by someone in the North last spring. I brought them back in tiny two-inch pots, and now I have spread them far and wide.

Another of my favorites for indoors is the velvet plant with the official name of *Gynura Aurantiaca*. The interestingly shaped leaves with their many points are covered with purple hairs. When looked at head-on they are green, but when viewed from the side they are purple. They suggest the changeable silks that our grandmothers used to wear. The prayer plant (maranta) is well-loved for the house. Its green leaves have darker green spots each side of a mid-rib that turns chocolate color as the leaf matures. One of the charms of the plant is responsible for its name. At night all the leaves fold upward, suggestive of arms raised in supplication. Maranta loves our rainy summers in the garden. And now when I bring it in, at the heart it flaunts a number of pencil-thin tightly furled new leaves. These will soon unwrap themselves into more patterned foliage.

All day we have been driving along beside fields of ripening cotton. At one point we stopped the car to walk through the rows. We'd never seen ripening cotton before. How beautiful the plants are, and many as tall as we. Blossoms white or cream open at the top. In the middle of the bush round fat pods are preparing to burst wide. At the bottom the pods have already sprung open to reveal bundles of soft, snowy cotton. Here row on row, stretching as far as we could see, grow potential sheets and towels, dresses, napkins, braided rugs, and curtains. In these days of synthetics it's a particular pleasure to see something growing out of the earth that will be used in many ways by all people everywhere, something as basic and indispensable as cotton. Of course, we had to pick a few stalks of the fluffy white bolls to take home.

In all the small towns we were passing through we drove by cotton gins where wisps of white were caught here and there in the most complicated and fascinating looking machinery. We kept meeting large trucks piled high with baled cotton. This cotton raising and harvesting was all a new experience to us.

Bob and I were returning from the coast, from Pawley's Island, where we had been staying for a week in a primitive little inn on the beach. We have a great fondness for the sea, and occasionally leave our beloved mountains for a visit to the shore. There are many possibilities in both North and South Carolina. Sometimes we camp in our tent-trailer, but this time we chose an inn. Our room looked out over the sand and sea and we lived day and night with the sound of the breakers.

About twenty years ago we sent to the Pawley's Island Hammock Shop for one of those marvelous large rope hammocks that have since become well known. We had replaced it several times as it wore out, and now we wanted to see where these wonderful works of art had originated.

The island itself is a strip of land with a beautiful wide sandy beach on the outer side and endless marshes on the inner side. A single road runs down the middle of the island from one end to the other. Along the beach and nestled in the dunes are countless weathered beach houses where you can envision families coming for gay summer holidays. In the marshes at low tide graceful white herons arrive to dine. Occasionally you are surprised by the nubbly back of a half-submerged alligator. We had taken books and I my sewing and we spent a good part of the week relaxing under a bright umbrella on the sand. The umbrella was covered with a design of huge pink roses which were most interesting if a little incongruous there by the sea. We were in and out of the very warm water and watching various shore birds. Now and then a shower of little fish, silver in the sunlight, would be tossed through the air as a wave crest folded over to break. We also saw the ominous black fin of a shark one day which made us both a little nervous.

We walked miles along the firm white sand. The beach was particularly lovely at night under the stars. A thrilling climax to our holiday came toward the end of our stay. We were wandering up the shore after dark when we came upon a line of small turtles heading from their nest toward the sea. These appealing creatures, fresh out of an egg, and perhaps three or four inches long, were emerging from a hole in the sand at the foot of one of the dunes. We stood spellbound, watching. Their first encounter with the world seemed to find them a little dazed as they struggled through the sand. But then, with that miraculous instinct of all creatures of the wild, they picked up their destiny and headed in a long line to the water. At first they started slowly, almost feebly, but every few yards they seemed to gather vitality and momentum. We couldn't resist picking up a couple and turning them away from the sea up the beach—but they promptly swung right around again! By the time they got down to where the sand was damp they were bundles of energy, vigor and vitality, their little flippers moving so fast they were all but trotting. When you put your hand on the sand in front of one it would go right around it and straight for the sea again. *Nothing* diverted them. We stood there in wonder and watched perhaps a hundred go out into the waves. Imagine being four inches long, encased in a shield, and viewing for the first time a world of sand, stars, and sea.

Next morning we went to the library and

lost ourselves in half a dozen intriguingly musty encyclopedias. Here we found out that the turtles were loggerheads, and that at maturity they weigh three to four hundred pounds. A single mating of these fabulous creatures fertilizes several seasons' eggs. On the night of the full moon in July the mother turtle comes ashore. This is her single annual emergence from the sea. With her flippers she hollows out the sand to form a nest a foot or so deep and there she lays a couple of hundred leathery-shelled eggs, each a little smaller than a golf ball. Carefully she covers them all with sand, then treks back to the water, giving her children-to-be no further thought or maternal care. The sun beating down on the sand incubates the eggs that hatch sixty to seventy days later. The baby turtles emerge in the dark of the moon, always, and go immediately back to the sea. An added mystery is the fact that when they mature they return to this same spot to lay eggs.

How do they breathe through all the sand before they reach the air? What becomes of the shells? We saw none. How do they ever know how to get to the sea? We were full of questions. And then all of a sudden our questions and curiosity ceased and we purely felt and appreciated the privilege of having experienced that evening's miracle. The whole instinctual side of nature is such an exciting business it makes good thinking and pondering in contemplative moments.

I'm fascinated by the different life-styles of us human beings. What endless variety there is in a group of people and their individual ways. This makes all relationships so interesting. In addition, within each individual how many differences—how many different selves we each of us possess. Wife and mother, neighbor, gardener, writer. On another level I have a self that loves exploring unfamiliar back-country roads, that doesn't like rush, pressure, and large noisy crowds. Another self that loves to dig and plant, that loves to read, that enjoys listening to good music, and yet another that likes walking in the woods. I could go on forever. We all have dozens of different selves. Perhaps a person could be likened to an orchestra with the basic Self as conductor. This sets the real Self a little apart from these other subpersonalities. It is up to us as conductor to integrate all the different parts of ourselves into a harmonious whole. Some of these selves we like better than others. Some we may be proud of. Some we may be ashamed of. Actually, seldom is anyone all good or all bad. There's usually something good about each one, and something less than good. However, we would probably never want any particular one to take over our lives, lest we become quite unbalanced. I would not like to always garden, always listen to music, always do anything, I guess. Surely we all need change and balance. None of the selves can be ignored. All need to be accepted as a very real part of us, and blended into a rhythmic whole.

We were in San Francisco last summer and attended an Esalen seminar on psychosynthesis. This approach to psychology was developed by a brilliant Italian, Dr. Roberto Assagioli. The name psychosynthesis may seem a bit unwieldy but the subject matter is completely absorbing. It was here, along with a lot of other stimulating things, that we learned this concept of the selves. The Self that directs the orchestra, it seems, is our Trans-personal Self, "that of God in every man," the Quakers would say. This Self has the ability to guide and control all these other selves. As the conductor of a symphony draws out first one group of musicians and then another, so we can manage and draw the best from all these numerous subselves.

The need to keep the different selves in hand is to be aware of the overall music being played, of theme and rhythm. And we never want to forget the Composer. The whole concept of the selves is useful in innumerable ways. When an ornery Self threatens to submerge us and throw us off base—in other words, when we get into a real messy emotional state about something as at times we all do—we can learn to withdraw and view the situation and see exactly what we are doing and what is happening. When we can, from the thick of them, observe our emotions, actions, and feelings from a little apart—and dispassionately—the heat cools and we can step onto firm ground again.

At Esalen we also learned some new aspects of energy. Any feeling a person has, good or bad, is a firm vigorous bundle of energy. The stronger the feeling, the more energy lies in it. This energy needs and *must have* expression. As I become aware of certain feelings and see them as a Self that I'm not proud of, no matter. The feeling is the thing I must deal with. And it is as real as any material object in our houses.

How many times have I said to myself, "This negative feeling is not significant in this situation. There is so much else that is positive about it. I'll forget the negative." So I would ignore the negative and shove it down inside, feeling virtuous. Now, since that summer I realize, while I don't have to dwell with the negative indefinitely, I must look it squarely in the eye. I must accept that these are *my* feelings of the moment, no matter how much I dislike and regret them, *or* decide they are justified. I need to know that the energy that lies in these emotions needs expression. I don't have to break furniture or make someone unhappy by losing my temper or handing out a lot of criticism to let off steam. There are other ways. I can go dig in the garden, turn out a few cupboards, bake a cake, or visit a loved and trusted friend and share it all with her. The main thing is the *recognition* of destructive feelings, the *acceptance* of them as part of me, for the moment at least, and the effort to release the negative energy into a positive vein before it settles way down in and corrodes. This is what we learned at Esalen. Of course, it isn't always easy or *even possible* to do this. The thing is to try, and I hope I'm learning.

The positive feelings and enthusiasms that rise up in us must find outlet just as much as the negatives or we will be in equal trouble. It's quite pleasant I find, when you appreciate someone, to tell them about it or express it in some definite way. When full of inspiration, how freeing and satisfying to write it, carry it out, and follow through on it someway. If you have a great urge to do something nice for someone, do it as soon as possible. Never stifle or postpone the feelings you have for positive action any more than the negatives.

The quality I like to feel stirring in me is the willingness to take risks. Some days it is near the surface and others it is buried deep and I cling to the familiar, the tried and true. Taking risks doesn't always lead to comfort but it invariably leads to aliveness and happenings. The willingness to venture forth, and I'm not thinking only in physical areas, opens us to new directions and ways. By taking risks we are committing ourselves to being willing to feel, to being hurt maybe, and in any case to exploring something new, some new path, inner or outer.

When you take a risk you are vulnerable and can be badly hurt, but you can also experience peaks of ecstasy and quiet joy. You are very much alive. To be vulnerable, and we're all vulnerable in certain areas, is to be moldable, flexible, adaptable, able to receive, able to change, and willing to consider the new and unfamiliar. Pity the person who has everything figured out and doesn't want to experience anything unexpected or different. There are such people, many of them, alas. In contrast, there are those who take risks and welcome the unexpected even if it is painful. But all of us, including we who think we are open and ready for anything, have somewhere in us a hidden area of our being, a hard little core that doesn't want any change at all. We may all have this in a different part of us. I'll admit that quite often I stub my toe on my hard core.

There are countless ways of taking risks. When we listen quietly, unprotestingly, and with interest to a point of view quite different from our own is one. We deserve a special medal if we can refrain from feeling we must persuade our friend to think our way. One who is confident in his own beliefs doesn't have to convert others to his views.

Taking risks keeps you out at the growing edge of living and brings a freshness to your days. A friendship or any relationship with such a person is an alive and exciting experience. One can, of course, take too many risks, be too open and vulnerable. One can be too anything. But mixed with the balance and stability that comes, hopefully, in being an adult, the willingness to take risks is a priceless treasure, one to cultivate and hold on to.

Bob participates in a men's discussion group that meets for luncheon on Thursdays. Recently all were asked to bring their own definition of religion. I particularly like Bob's for its simplicity and depth.

Religion is the belief in a Power beyond
    the human
The search to understand that Power
The effort to live by it.

Banks brought me the most beautiful parsley plant. It is as lovely as any fern could be, and comes from an outdoor garden. Fresh new leaves stand up in the center and streamers of long stalks of green trail down, fernlike, around the pot. Her instructions were to cut these off and a new plant would emerge at the center. But they are so beautiful I cannot trim them yet. Next week I shall have a meat loaf, and it calls for a cup of chopped parsley so I shall use them then.

My chives from outdoors is also flourishing. The basil cuttings have been in that glass of water two weeks now and all have roots. I've potted them up for friends and for ourselves.

Out in the garden I'm giving away impatiens cuttings to those who want to root them. We had despaired of the seven figs, concluding that they were not going to ripen this season, when all of a sudden the largest one began to soften and develop a slightly roseate tone. So again we dream of figs—or maybe *a* fig for breakfast.

The chrysanthemums are now a riot of color, even this year's cuttings are flowering. They are golden-brown shades, yellows, mauves, reds, and some tiny pompom yellows.

Wayside Garden bulbs have arrived and yesterday we planted daffodils. Bob digs the holes and I put six or seven bulbs in each one. They are large and flourishing, many being two together. I love setting out bulbs. A promise lies in each one, an appointment with the future. In the terrace garden, where we can see them from the living room, I'm also digging in crocuses, chionodoxa, iris, reticulata and winter aconite, hoping I have put in the latter right-side-up. As we plant, our imaginations run wildly ahead, envisioning the fairyland of next spring's garden. Spring begins in February here with a few hints the month ahead in the yellow January jasmine and snowdrops.

Beautiful and exciting October is drawing to a close. The temperature is dropping. For two nights we have brought our geraniums in. Each flower head is large as a grapefruit—almost. We cannot bear to think of them frosted. Last night there was a frost in many of our neighbors' gardens, but it was thirty-six degrees here. We are sure this is because our house and garden stand in the Thermal Belt—the mysterious area that winds along through the mountains and holds off the frost.

Today our breath fogged as we were walking and we had to move fast to keep warm; I wore my woolen mittens. By late morning it was warm in the sun. In the woods everywhere a kind of golden glow permeates the very air itself as sunlight is reflected from the turning foliage. The reds and yellows are coming, and the maroon dogwood shades are deepening. Tulip leaves are gradually losing their green and we know that next month they will be a bright, sunny yellow along with the maples. While the show of color is still in the early stages, each branch somewhere is a little different from the way it was an hour ago.

All month hard little acorns have been dropping onto the terrace bricks, periodically, each with a sharp little plop. We hear them landing on the roof too. The squirrels are busy, busy burying acorns all through the garden. Planting little forests. Do they remember where they dig them all in? How could they? Many will grow and next spring we shall be pulling up potential oak forests. Relaxing on the terrace, I watch a squirrel climb up the oak—get its acorn—come down to bury it, and then up for another!

The season that began to change a little in September is really different now, and summer and all the warm weather activities are pleasant memories. Each morning the birds flock to the feeders, chickadees scalloping through the air almost before it is light, then the tufted titmouse, sleek and trim; the nuthatch, the woodpeckers—downy and hairy—the cardinals, in pairs usually. Most dramatic of all the pileated woodpecker. He clings to the far side of the trunk of the oak and reaches his head shyly around for suet, and at the first sign of movement in a window anywhere he is off. A very timid creature.

This morning began so gayly before breakfast. Del, our brother-in-law, called from Columbus, Ohio, to tell us that he was cooking seven-grain cereal for breakfast and could find only six grains! We have a sort of standing joke and teasing back and forth on organic foods and vitamins. We go in for them and they do not, but they did like this cereal when visiting us, and succumbed just that far organically, but no farther, please!

While Del and Bob were talking, I came in with a handful of chives from the window garden for the crepes that Bob was going to make. I added a word to Kay and Del before we all hung up. I had also brought in the strawberry harvest: one beautiful red berry about three-quarters of an inch long and a third of an inch thick. We cut it in two and each had half. What a morsel of deliciousness. I am looking ahead to next summer because the plants are flourishing, really burgeoning!

After breakfast we went to the discussion group that meets at church before the service. It was one of those days when I felt extremely open and responsive. Everything said everywhere seemed to speak to *me*.

How good to see friends and neighbors and exchange a word and a warmth with each. Also to meet and welcome newcomers. I remember how lonely we were when we first came, and how much it meant when people were especially friendly toward us as all were.

In the afternoon I took off my good clothes and put on my full Mexican skirt. For some reason I always feel carefree when I wear this skirt. It is full, a little long and such a dreamy violet color. I guess it stirs the gypsy in me. Surely we all have a touch of the spirit of these wild folk lurking somewhere within.

We drove through Dark Corners and parked and walked to Twin Lakes. It was an enchanted afternoon. First a little chipmunk had rushed across the road in front of us. He skittered fast and close to the ground, that little bundle of vibrant life bent on chipmunk business. As we walked along, listening to the stream on one side, we heard a rustling in the bushes and there alongside the dirt road were a family of quail slipping off through the trees—but not until we had had a good look at the children moving close together over the fallen leaves behind their mother.

All at once we came upon a persimmon tree. We picked up a few delicious sweet deadripe fruits lying on the ground under it. They look dirty and unappetizing, but are terribly good after you brush off the dirt and summon the courage to bite into one. Their goodness, like much in living, is a matter of timing. When exactly ripe and ready they are never puckery but always a sweet morsel!

At the first of Twin Lakes we stopped as usual and stretched out on the weathered gray wooden dock in the sunlight. The mountains, Hogback, Rocky Spur, and Melrose, our special three, seemed near enough to touch, and how blue were the shadows in the folds of their contours and how bright the colors up their slopes. If we feel we come near to God in church, and we do, we *know* we touch Him out here under the sky in the shadow of the mountains!

Lying on the dock we watched two ducks swimming around the surface, now toward each other, now apart in a kind of dance. One would fly up, circle about and settle on the water again; then his partner would do the same. It was still, and the mirroring of surrounding trees in the water was never lovelier. In the brilliant sun they seemed to have gold haloes. The whole reflection in the still, still water was like a French Impressionist painting. Like a Seurat, loose and soft with rims of light bordering every shape. I have seldom seen anything more meltingly beautiful. I was envisioning how I would like to paint the scene. Then I stopped. This is the painting, like many others, that will remain in my head, something never to forget that I will draw out on days when spirits dip. I have many experiences for use this way. I also bring them out when spirits are high too. For at any time they make pleasant ruminating!

After lying on the dock a while we headed back. And along the roadside picked armfuls of the last goldenrod, purple asters, tiny white daisies, and other roadside flowers for a fresh bouquet beside the front door.

11

November Is Kinds of Light

WE are walking along a wood road on persian-carpet colors, reds, scarlets, and rich coppery tones, while beams of sun come filtering down through the tall trees. It poured last night, a hard, hard rain, at times pounding on the roof with such force I wondered if the house would slide down the hillside into the brook! Today the large trunks of pines, hemlocks, tulip trees and oaks that rise in great perpendiculars are still wet and black. Tinted foliage, shiny from the rain, gathers up the sunlight and sends a dazzle through the woods. Everywhere leaves are gently falling. In streaks of color they drift down, and with a soft sighing sound settle on the forest floor. Many of these trees were here long ago, when the occasional little cabins along our trail, each in its own clearing, were new. In those days there was red mud stuffed between the logs instead of the cement that we see now.

Surely this is the peak of autumn. The colors couldn't be more vivid, we agree, admiring a golden maple tangled in with a red sourwood. We've been saying this every day, and each morning a new climax is reached and all outdoors has become still more dramatic. Yet here are certain maples still brilliant green, the last to turn, a mere hint of red or yellow rimming one or two leaves.

To get to where we are we had driven across the railroad tracks, the main line up into the mountains and on to Asheville and, they say, the steepest railroad grade this side of the Mississippi. What a beautiful train ride it was when cars carried passengers instead of the freight of today. It was a leisurely trip because they used to stop whenever the passengers wanted to pick flowers. As long as the engineer got in before dark he was in no hurry. I remember coming down here some years ago when our daughter, Joan, was sixteen. It was February so there were no flowers, but we each had a bike and took the train huffing and puffing seven miles up the mountain.

Then we had the exhilarating joy of coasting all the way down the hairpin turns back to Tryon.

The winding road where we are traveling today leads up along the side of Melrose Mountain, past an old abandoned vineyard, presently changing from paving to dirt. Where the lane narrows we leave the car and follow along on foot high on the slope of the valley. If we go far enough we will reach Melrose Falls. Occasionally we glimpse, on the valley floor, a string of tiny cars. From this height they seem to be merely inching along up toward the town of Saluda. The name Saluda is from the Indian *Saluta*, meaning River of Corn, an apt description of many of the coves and valleys in midsummer. The corn in the fields, row on row, with tassels waving in the breeze, actually does seem to flow. From this wild beauty on the slope of Melrose Mountain the cars below seem incongruous and insignificant. There is a here-today-and-gone-tomorrow feeling about them, these man-made machines. In contrast, we raise our eyes to the whole range beyond, Tryon Mountain, Big and Little Warriors, White Oak, and all in their giddiest of colors. The automobiles, now hidden by a bend in the trail, melt right out of awareness. We and the mountain stand alone together.

And now comes the sound of water and there ahead tumbles a fresh mountain stream, pouring over great rocks in a small gorge. We must step from boulder to boulder to cross as the water sweeps over the road. In this exquisite little green gorge masses of tall rhododendron tower up into the trees, along with laurel and fern. Beyond, we come upon a whole mountainside of Christmas fern. How graceful are the rich green arching fronds, with each little pinna shaped like a Christmas stocking. Here is one plant growing in the sheltering roots of a tree trunk, partly spilling over a neighboring gray rock—a rock patterned with green moss, soft to touch.

We started out briskly, looking at our watches, but by now we have lost all sense of time and, consequently, are able to listen to the forest and what it has to tell us. Walking in woods, ideas occur and develop that seldom come to mind anywhere else. I see different answers to problems, my own and those of the universe. And frequently touches of cosmic philosophy drift my way through the trees. Our pace slows, our senses awaken to further wonders everywhere. Here sprawls a great bank of partridgeberry covered with little round red fruits. We gather a few stems for a terrarium. And now a dusty pink maple-leaved viburnum reaches out from a rocky ledge, the soft leaves almost velvety to touch. On all sides the smell of the forest rises. Woods scents differ at every season. The fragrance of fall is a mix of dry leaves, fresh mountain streams, damp, rich earth.

Standing beside the trail is a great old chestnut stump, worn and rotted by the sun and storms of many seasons. It emerges from the ground, a miniature medieval castle like those along the Rhine. For moments I lose myself in the many little turrets and winding trails and secret mossy gardens formed in the old wood stump. These chestnut remains are everywhere cradling in their disintegrating centers fresh new trees, tall and slim, but not, alas, chestnuts. And thus today has its roots in yesterday and is nourished by what was.

We pause for a rest. My sight wanders

up a tall tulip tree exploring various branches on the way. The tipmost leaves, catching the sun, shimmer in the breeze, while the glow of all the gold foliage illumines the very air.

We have arrived at the old Pentecostal Holiness church, today a mere ruin in the woods with a small overgrown graveyard beside it. On the downhill side the tumbling building is still supported by three piles of flat rocks. Windows are broken, the floor falling apart, and the roof partly caved in. But the altar, a simple wooden stand, remains. parts of two pews are left. How straight-backed these are, and how uncompromisingly hard to sit on.

I settled down in the sunny doorway to wait while Bob explored the road farther on. Alone with the past, I sense the presence of those who came to worship and can envision people gathering. Now comes a horse and buggy jogging along, bringing a whole family to church. They would tether the horse just there, perhaps. And now another family draws near, walking. Here is a young couple, the man carrying a small baby. Then there appears an old man, at the other end of life, and moving slowly with a cane.

Lingering there on the church steps I recalled the story they tell about an itinerant preacher here in the mountains who, when he could leave his farm, used to travel many miles to different churches to preach. One of his neighbors once asked him how much he got for his services. The astonished reply was, "I don't get nothing. It takes all of them as long to come and hear me as it takes to preach. The least I can do if they take the trouble to come, is to preach to them."

After a few minutes Bob returned, bringing me back to today. Heading homeward we looked down into the valley where the Pacolet River runs, gathering unto itself all the streams along its route. In the mountains a stream is called a "branch." River beds and roads used to be one and the same in the days when roads were scarce. A river bed made a bumpy road to be sure, and a wet one at times, but a way to get through. Traveling along a tunnel of green with tree branches meeting overhead must have been quite beautiful.

Needs were fewer and life simpler in

these mountain coves and valleys a hundred years ago, or even fifty. A mountain man was able to satisfy most of his wants and needs from his own land in his own private clearing. He was well content with this state of affairs. There's a serene and peaceful atmosphere in an area where for generations people were able to get most of their needs from the earth.

Walking back to the car, we passed one particular log cabin with various sheds and a large garden which belongs to the Burrells. Many years ago when we were here on a holiday I was riding horseback along this same road with our daughter, Joan, then age five. She was on a small shaggy brown pony. That morning is etched in my memory, never to be forgotten. A train whistle startled the pony. In an instant Joan had tumbled to the ground and I was off my horse and beside her. I was comforting her tears and exploring to be sure that nothing was broken. I found only a few splinters from a log where her hand had stopped the fall. Meanwhile a mountain woman came out of the cabin, a Mrs. Burrell of a bygone era, followed by a dog, two cats and three small children, each child with long blond hair in pigtails.

What I have remembered all these years was Mrs. Burrell's kindly warmth, concern and brisk efficiency. Before I hardly knew what happened she had Joan on her lap. Out of an apron pocket she drew a bit of sewing and removed the needle with which she deftly took the splinters from the child's hand. I still remember her gentle skill and her caring and that of her children who stood quietly in a circle, watching.

In sharp contrast to the simpler lives of the mountain families years back, and their freedom from gadgets, come the annual fall gift catalogues. Every mail brings more. We cannot imagine how we got on so many lists, but still they arrive. Of course, some are helpful and welcome and we tuck these in a drawer and frequently order from them. But enough is enough and we really get too many! How hard the cataloguers must work to think up something new and different. For example, leafing through the pages of a recent arrival, here's an electric clock that casts large numerals on the ceiling all night so if you waken you don't need to move even your head but only open one eye to know what the hour is!

How many aids are here for keeping your pets happy. Here's an umbrella to attach to your dog's leash to keep him dry as you walk him in the rain, and what's more it comes in a variety of shades and patterns. Do you pick his favorite color? On some chilly night, you can slip your feet into an electric toe-toaster. Or would you like a chenille cotton rug, the pattern being an enlarged replica of a hundred-dollar bill, complete with Benjamin Franklin, and the suggestion in the catalogue caption, "Here's a hundred-dollar bill you can throw around!" I am sensing Mr. Franklin shuddering in his grave. On the next page I discover two absolutely sinister cast-aluminium barefoot-shaped car pedals —each toe separated. These you clamp over your existing pedals. "This zingy new accessory puts the barefoot gypsy look inside your car." Just what we all need!

In this era when we sometimes have the panicky feeling that civilization is trying to de-personalize us with crowds, condominiums and vast supermarkets, it's comforting to find in the pages at hand all the numerous things that you can buy personalized. For example, I cannot wait to own a set of multicolored powderpuffs, each with my name on it! Would these Christmas tree ornaments, marked with our names, give us a sense of self-worth and importance in our crowded world? Or would they let us think somebody cared if we felt lonely on Christmas day?

Here are personalized mats for the floor of the car, "his" and "hers," or your own name permanently molded in. I discover personalized doormats, door knockers, pipes, tobacco pouches, cigarettes, pajamas (in case you forget who you are in the night?), tote bags, teacups, hangers. Here is a pen, with your name on it of course, but even more: it is guaranteed to write satisfactorily not only on earth but also in outer space! So if you find it failing, you can return it from Mars. It also promises to write for three consecutive miles. This, we are told, is four times longer than an ordinary pen.

I'm really excited by the pill-tote, which has a time-indicator on each bottle cap that goes off when you're supposed to take the pill, and records that you have taken it.

Now I can picture myself walking over the lawn, wearing a pair of the spiked-heeled sandals from another page, which in some unfathomable manner will mow, aereate, water and feed the grass simultaneously. While engaged in this fourfold process I hear a little bell ring in my pocket and realize I have to take the next pill. It all might be too much and I'd have to take to bed beneath a crystal chandelier that I may screw into any ceiling socket like a light bulb. I wouldn't really have a good night's rest, though, unless I had that fragrant nightlight. The warmth of the bulb fills the air all night long with the delicate essence of spring. What about summer, fall and winter? Horrors, what if I waken at midnight and don't know what season it is!

Once you get to lamps the catalogue has really lost its head. Here is one: a clear glass globe, filled with bright blue-green iridescent lavalike bubbles which continually move and change the pattern. It is thirty-one ninety-five and promises to be very soothing. I wonder.

How could a fisherman get on without a personalized floating fish knife shaped like a fish? And how could a writer survive without a pencil sharpener made like an old-fashioned telephone? While you ring the bell the pencil sharpens.

Each page has something on it that seems to outdo the previous page. Here is a "Melody Phone"—a gadget, pink if you like, to attach to your telephone. When the steak burns, or the washing machine overflows, or the doorbell rings in the middle of your phone conversation, just press the button and music entertains your friend at the other end of the wire while you solve the crisis. He or she can listen to Ave Maria or Oh, What a Beautiful Morning. I can just see myself coping with burned steaks, Fuller Brush salesmen at the door, sheets running over the floor from an overflowing washer, to the cheerful words "the corn is as high as an elephant's eye . . ."

I thought this was just about the peak of inanity when I came across the Executive Decision-Maker. This is so phenomenal I don't know if I can even describe it. It's sort of a hollow, Lucite X-shaped object filled with fluid and a small, floating ball. It stands on two legs. At the top of one leg is the word "Yes"; at the top of the other the word "No". When the harassed executive has a great decision to make, he can save himself from ulcers by setting down this little gadget on his desk so that the ball is at the bottom. Then he watches it drift upward. When the ball—decision-maker—reaches the crossing of the X it will go either toward YES or NO, thus relieving the executive of all responsibility. Vast and weighty problems are completely solved for a mere ten dollars!

I do enjoy the Garden Club here in Tryon. Each month we gather in a different member's house and every place seems to have its own special and superb mountain view. What wonderful refreshments we have. It is pleasant communing with the various members too. All are interesting and congenial and as in any group all delightfully different. Recently a fine Japanese speaker gave a particularly fascinating lecture on flower arranging. When he used a leaf with a hole in it in one bouquet someone questioned him: "Shouldn't a perfect leaf be there instead?"

"No," the gracious gentleman replied, "Hole in leaf not bad—man can always go through hole. Man never blocked, never prisoner. Always way out with hole in leaf. Man needs way out."

At the last garden club meeting the speaker brought along for all of us several dozen paper cups, each one planted with a Christmas rose seedling from her garden. After I had set ours out in a spot prepared with ample plant food and leaf mold from the woods, I was charmed to run across a legend of how the Christmas rose came to be.

Among those coming to worship the baby Jesus was a little ten-year-old girl who had no money and who had walked a great distance. When she arrived, tired, at the door of the stable she saw others coming with gifts and began to cry because she had nothing to offer. Her tears dropped on the earth beside the door where she stood and there sprang up on the instant a flourishing plant—the first Christmas rose, covered with snowy white blossoms. This small child, awed by the miracle and delighted by the flowers, picked a bouquet and, refreshed and smiling, entered to lay her gift at the feet of the newborn Christ child.

Summer is a season of outer activity and things constantly happening. Fall is the time we gradually move indoors, a time of friends and fires and quiet ruminating. What better place to ruminate than looking into the flames or embers of burning wood? Open fires send forth fine fragrances. The scent fills the whole house. Step outdoors and the smoke coming out the chimney has a very special smell.

We are able to buy little bundles of fat pine here. With these small sticks you never need paper: merely touch a match to them, they flare up and burn.

The mountain people have their own ingenious way of lighting fires. They absolutely scorn the use of paper, ever. A mountain man will take a stick and skillfully whittle it into a fine brush. He never fails to get his fire started from these beginnings with one match, be it indoors or out.

We have a fireplace in the living room and one in the bedroom. The latter is a small wall fireplace and from bed we are able to watch the miniature logs burn down to embers as we drift off to sleep.

Living in the woods we are learning about trees. How differently various wood burns. The oak tree expresses itself as characteristically in the way it burns as it does in its leaves and fruits. Different varieties of oaks behave differently. The white oak has a serene and quiet blaze. Spanish oak logs spit and explode and the way the sparks shoot out you must be ever alert unless you have a good tight screen.

A steadfast glow emerges from lighted hickory. The chestnut, which we don't have these days, is said to have been as full of sputters and pops as a Spanish oak. If you are using linwood the open fire will be alive with families of fierce orange dragons that leap about, lashing their tails in the air. Apple logs create a warm and quiet fire, sending up flames of blue and yellow. Burning cherry wood smells of flowers. Black gum behaves quietly, tossing up darting, pointed flames.

It's interesting to see if we can recognize a tree when its wood is alight. Is it oak, pine, hickory? Could any one of us ever develop the mountain man's sensitivity to trees and be able to recognize the variety we are walking under on a summer night by the sound of the wind through the foliage?

You can see so much more in a fire than merely wood burning and warmth emanating, satisfying as this may be. How old was this tree and what were some of its experiences in life? Where did it stand in the forest? How did the buds smell in the spring? In your mind the logs before you rebuild themselves into a great tree. Maybe in some dreamy mood, especially if you have been reading fairy stories to grandchildren lately, you can see the tree as imprisoning a dryad or nymph or woodland sprite for a generation or two. Now, in the burning, these confined elfin creatures are suddenly loosed, emerging into a kind of elemental freedom. Up through the flame tips they go and out, back to their forest homes—and all because Bob went to our hillside with his saw and his axe and created a beautiful woodpile. And because we are now entering the season of using it.

Elizabeth Goudge writes, "You love a new home because it stands there waiting to be good to humans, and an old one because it has already been good to humans." Our house was ten years old when we bought and remodeled it three years ago. So it is both old and new. It had already been good to its former inhabitants; it is being good to us now.

Much of living involves responses, those we give and those we receive. I am thinking of home and all it means. You build a brick terrace, and it gives you wonderful hours outdoors. A small fat toad comes and lives there, dozing on the bricks in the shade of a gardenia bush. You plant azaleas and camellias and they reward you with clusters of flowers, each in season. You feed them, and they grow and flourish. The fig tree, watered and fed and mulched, responds with fruit.

You wash windows and sunshine streams through the clear clean glass. In the kitchen you mix up a lot of different ingredients, often fragrant. You put them in the oven and the result is a lovely cake, or delicious pie, or muffins, or soufflés. Of course, sometimes things in the oven go down instead of up! Life has always its vagaries which serve to keep us alert.

Home and our relation to it is a constant

matter of giving and receiving. In the receiving phase of this exchange a home seems to become a part of you, almost like an outer skin. Where you live, be it a house or an apartment, soon becomes an out-picturing of you who live there. Home seeps into your senses, the heart and mind and emotions become inevitably entangled. As you pour love and caring into your home, they are returned with interest, and seemingly whenever you need them most. I revel in the sense of being where I belong when we sit by the fire on a cool evening, listening to records, reading aloud, or each engrossed in his own book, or out under the stars on the terrace, or in the kitchen preparing a meal. I have this same feeling of rightness when I waken in the morning and listen to the trill of a single bird in a treetop. I feel it when I fall asleep at night hearing the gentle and familiar sounds that I have learned belong in our home, the cuckoo clock, the gentle purring of the utilities.

Recently, when digging bulbs into the garden, I became aware of the sound of the brook down our woodland slope. Merging with the music of tumbling water was the soft swish of the breeze through the trees. With the sensitivity to these familiar evidences of belonging here, came that best feeling of all—the awareness of the earth, the land, and of a great, undergirding strength. The earth is our right place, though the heavens, broad and vast, ever beckon. The more firmly we are grounded, the higher we can soar. But though all that happens we are never beyond the touch of earth.

What is your favorite flower? people often ask me. And my answer I am sure marks me as rather spineless because I tell the truth and say I like the one that is blooming at the moment. If this makes me characterless, well, then so it does. But now, as the bush of white camellias outside the front door is opening new buds daily, and the one near it is a riot of beautiful valentine-pink flowers with tufted yellow centers I know I like camellias best. But when I go outside the fence and look at the chrysanthemums flowering there, in all their lovely tawny shades—violet, rusty orange, bright yellow, red single ones, and myriad more—I realize that these are my best loved.

Yet I know full well that next spring, when the white hyacinths planted this fall are in bloom, sending their fragrance far and wide, I shall be sure that those are my favorites of all time. And so it goes the year round.

I guess the matter of seasons is the same thing. I am sure now that I like this delirious, mad, marvelous month of November best. Fall is a miracle of beauty. Fall, when nature dumps her whole palette of colors over the landscape, and trails mists through purple valleys at dusk.

When spring comes? We shall see. But this moment I am caught in the spell of autumn.

November is kinds of light. Candlelight, firelight, and leaves falling and letting more light into the forests. November is also starlight, how the stars sparkles this month. November is moonlight, too.

Moonlight and starlight. Moonlight tells you things, shows you details that starlight merely hints at. Starlight suggests, starlight is might-be, perhaps, maybe, sometimes.

Moonlight is here and now. Sometimes the mood of moonlight captures us; sometimes that of starlight. I like both. Often I want to receive outright, other times I need to seek what I can barely discern. Occasionally I want to follow a hint, other days I have to see a definite shape.

Moonlight and starlight—life is a pleasant mix of both, one alternating with the other. Each comes at its own time with the turn of the earth, the swing of the heavens, the shape of the seasons.

Starlight is the other side of the mountain, the part you know is there but do not see. Moonlight the slope you are on, where you stand and look about you at what definitely is and now.

I am outside on the terrace in the starlight, alone, and moving as I feel the rhythm of the music that drifts from indoors. Suppé's *Poet and Peasant* overture.

Timing, rhythm, a sense of motion, being exactly *with* the music, a oneness, a connectedness with something that is great, greater than myself. Something vast as the heavens above, that permeates the earth, that emerges in a thousand visible ways, in the perfect curve of a pine cone or of a lone wave, the wet scallop shapes where breakers wash a sandy beach, the turn of the tide, the design of a small snail shell, the shape of a single egg in a wild bird's nest.

And now suddenly, and all unknowing, the music and I part. I am moving still but I have lost everything. There is a separateness. I am alone, lonely. I am missing something—

A few moments later the melody picks me up again, and I am with it, completely, thoroughly. The lost is found, harmony restored. The rhythm tells me where and how to move. Communication direct from music to me; my limbs respond. No thought or word intrudes.

As I move and the music flows, again I feel the immensity, the sounds and cadences have caught and lifted me beyond, beyond notes, beyond time, beyond me.

I am a kite flying high. I am the wind, blowing softly. I am the stream, rushing at night over a bed of sand and stones. The stream, seeking and finding the river. I am that river, wandering, meandering, and reaching the sea, to loose itself, merging into something greater, broader, deeper.

I seek no longer. I am there. Where? In a moment of still perfection . . . time stops . . .

Moments later, I know not how many, comes a gradually sharpening awareness of my physical self moving about on the brick terrace, moving to music, moving in ways my body wants to move, with no conscious plan or pattern, no set dance. What freedom and joy I have experienced. I have traveled far and am back.

The touch of the earth has brought me home.

It is bedtime. Quiet—man's quiet is the overture to the sounds of nature. The sounds of the night, the rhythm of our stream down the hill, delicious peace.

Will the touch of the earth always bring me back? I hope so for I want it that way.

Everywhere leaves are falling and blowing about. These days we have lengthening vistas through the woods, climaxed here and there by a brilliant gold tulip tree, a dazzling red maple, and always the rosy copper oaks. As the leaves fall, we are gradually able to view the mountains through the trees. The full view arrives as the last leaf drifts to earth. We're just getting the first vistas now, a hint of what lies ahead. Early, early in the morning I can see a small piece of mountain, raspberry red at the tip from the first sun rays.

Beside our bathtub is an enormous window that reaches to the ceiling. Sitting in a nice warm bath we are in the treetops, since the bathroom is on the downhill side of the house. With leaves tumbling we must draw the curtain at night to be private, because by day our vista begins to reveal all the way through the woods to the road across the brook.

This is the time of year I particularly enjoy our kitchen, and certain favorite utensils. There is that pot that breathes. It's stainless steel with a copper bottom. When you simmer anything with the cover on, this cover rises and falls gently in its own special rhythm. To us it has become "the pot that breathes" and we always refer to it as such. There are other favorites. A large stirring spoon with a teak wood handle feels smooth and pleasant to the touch. An appealing characteristic of a kitchen is that it is a place of textures, a place where you feel and touch and are keenly aware.

So much of life, impressions, relationships and any kind of communication comes to us through our minds and intellects that it is always refreshing to leave the realm of thought and step into the areas of touch. In summer this occurs out in the garden as we dig and plant and prune and weed. The feel of the earth, the wet moisture after the rain and the different textures of various plants all make pleasant handling. But now, this season, I'm in the kitchen enjoying the feel of rising dough. I like to watch the bubbling up of batter and the feel of turning the pancakes over. What a nice texture has bread and toast. Many foods that you handle are good to touch. The firmness of a potato, the softness of a ripening avocado, the fluffiness of a head of Boston lettuce, the cool smoothness of a banana. I could go on and on. We each have our favorite aspects of our own kitchens. This in some way is the time of year when we draw strength and comfort from the things of home. And the kitchen is the heart and core of the home.

It is where things change and become—a place of continual transformation.

Rain can be a dull gray affair while you wait and long for sun. But tonight the rain is magic. Through the living-room windows we watch it fall in streaks of silver, shining in the glow of the outside light under the eaves. This light illumines the Japanese stone lantern, the wooden outside benches, the falling leaves like shapes of wet copper scattered over the brick terrace. Everything shines with wetness. We are in the living room in front of the fire. We are on the sofa facing the fireplace, eating off trays; sipping tomato bisque along with dark brown bread and baked apples. The flames reach up in streaks of fire, tongues of brightness. What vitality and vigor in a wood fire—how alive it is. It talks to us gently and we listen.

We drank our soup, finished up the apples, and settled to listen to music while I happily hooked my rug, with always half an eye out the window at the magic created by the rain falling on a wet, wet world.

November is the month of the church bazaars, and we enjoy them all. Last week was the first. The parish house was gala with decorations and quite a crowd waited outside in the sunlight for the doors to open at eleven. I headed immediately for the table of stuffed animals, having eight-year-old Galen in mind. He's the grandchild who loves animals and sleeps with so many there's hardly room for him in the bed. I had a hard time deciding between some velour frogs, stuffed with birdseed and with the consistency of a bean bag, and a bright red horse with flowing mane and tail of long, luscious white wool. But then my eye was caught and held by an old-gold-colored giraffe with pink spots and large eyes, wool eyelashes and a kind of wistful look! There was an irresistible cuddlyness about him and his wayward ears. And here, next to the giraffe, was the perfect apron, a charming blue and yellow print for Joan's birthday next week. Tucking the giraffe under my arm and coaxing Bob to put the apron in his pocket, we wandered over to the Baked Goods. How could we live without that sweet potato pie? We didn't even try, and why not freeze that mince pie for Thanksgiving? And look at this luscious lemon cake, and we have to buy these "lemon love notes"! What can they be? They look like small pastry sandwiches of lemon-pie filling one inch square! The world's best food turns up at these bazaars where everything is home-baked and seldom a mix involved. Pretty soon we both had to make a trip to the car with our loot. And back again.

As much fun as what you buy at the bazaars is seeing all your friends and stopping to talk to this one and that. So many skillfully made and attractive things were on the craft table. All in the community turn out their best for these occasions. I lost my heart to a little collection of tiny vases made of walnut, maybe three inches high, each one in a different shape. They had a tiny narrow hole in the top. Every one held a single stalk of a dried weed. Tracy had made them on his lathe, I knew, he being very skillful at building and making just about anything. Bob at my elbow selected a particularly graceful vase, slightly Greek in shape, and we added this to our collection.

The plane lights twinkled across the black night sky. Airports are gay before a holiday. Groups of young people going home from the nearby colleges crowd together laughing, talking. Long hair, jeans, the usual. Here and there, standing out against the rest, is a young man with a regular suit and short hair, or a college girl with hers neat and up. I do like to see the shape of young people's heads, their foreheads, necks and ears!

Now we are greeting and embracing Janet. Suitcases and bundles stowed, we drive home in the starlight.

One of our great joys here is having old friends from Connecticut and elsewhere in the North come for a visit. They usually arrive trailing bits of city pressures. When we moved here, we left an area of tension and rush. An exciting, stimulating section, to be sure, but one where people are busy, busy, and always hurrying. I guess we were that way too. Now it pleases us to watch our friends gently unwind when they come to visit us. How happy we are to observe them gradually melt and merge into the leisurely ways of our beloved small town where you don't count each minute or hour. So with Janet. She arrived from hurried, rushing days. We walked in the mountains, sat by the fire, talked, shared ideas and feelings, listened to records and caught up on the news of our erstwhile hometown and mutual friends.

One morning Bob made popovers that rose up and up. He truly outdid himself! On another day I made organic griddle cakes. Still another breakfast we had kippers and bran muffins.

A neighboring couple who are close friends joined us for Thanksgiving dinner, and arrived bearing gifts. Spiced peaches and pickled cucumbers they had made. Also a strawberry muffin mix I'd recently eaten at their house and loved. It was all in a grape basket sprayed with gala red spray. In the center of the Thanksgiving table stood a round silver bowl of our own white camellias with extra leaves spread out toward each one's place. We ate at five for the best enjoyment of candlelight and later a fire. Turkey, mashed potatoes and gravy, wine, and that marvelous bazaar sweet potato pie. How content I was with Bob there at the head of the table, me at the other end, and the mystic glow of candles between. I was feeling the warmth of having close friends together, new friends and an old friend. I was also musing on how, out beyond the walls of our house, neighbors were having their own time of appreciation, of home, family, and friends.

After dinner we gathered around the fire and I read part of one of my favorite poems. "The Great Lover" by Rupert Brooke. It speaks of all his loves including . . .

> . . . live hair that is
> Shining and free; blue-massing clouds;
>   the keen
> Unpassioned beauty of a great
>   machine;
> The benison of hot water; furs to
>   touch;
> The good smell of old clothes; and
>   other such—
> The comfortable smell of friendly
>   fingers,
> Hair's fragrance, and the musty reek
>   that lingers
> About dead leaves and last year's
>   ferns . . .
>
> . . . Sweet water's dimpling laugh from
>   tap or spring;
> Holes in the ground; and voices that do
>   sing;

Voices in laughter too; and body's pain,
Soon turned to peace; and the deep
     panting train;
Firm sands; the little dulling edge of
     foam
That browns and dwindles as the wave
     goes home;
And washen stones, gay for an hour;
     the cold
Graveness of iron; moist black earthen
     mold;
Sleep; and high places; footprints in
     the dew;
And oaks; and brown horse-chestnuts,
     glossy new;
And new peeled sticks; and shining
     pools on grass;
All these have been my loves.

We all took pencils and paper and wrote our own personal favorite loves. How different were the lists, each reflecting the person who wrote it. We shared these aloud amidst much laughter, joy, and wonder. And the conversation wandered on to other things in living we found especially meaningful, both tangibles and intangibles, things we were grateful for, while the fire turned to embers and time slid by.

The evening ended. Our neighbors went home. We three cleared up a little and turned out the lights.

On the way to sleep, listening to the wind in the pines and the murmur of the brook, further thoughts of thankfulness drifted my way. Surely thanksgiving is very much an inner experience. Appreciation grows and flourishes when shared, but has its birth in the private depths of each one of us. Some people, sad to say, find it impossible or uncomfortable to express or receive appreciation and gratitude, though I am sure everyone feels it. Perhaps it is mostly a by-product of what we are, what we have become and have allowed to develop in us. And always regardless of outer circumstances and material possessions. There is so much to be grateful for besides what we own—for just being, for each day —for sun and rain, and seasons; for camellias and friends and fires and curled-up kittens, for sunrises and trees. Lying there Thanksgiving night I went on adding to the list I'd made earlier with our friends, things that drifted into consciousness. Couldn't we all go on forever with such a list?

I remember a holiday in Guatemala and the *joie de vivre* we found in remote Indian villages where we saw many a whole family living in a one-room thatched hut with a dirt floor and almost no furniture. They owned a minimum of material possessions, these Guatemalans, yet what a love of life we felt in them, what gratitude for life itself.

A sense of thanksgiving, I believe, is even more than something we carry about inside; it shines out in our lives. It is fanned from ember to flame by our own way of being.

12

December Is the Month of Listening

"COULD I have a box?" I asked Mr. Cowan. "Certainly," he replied, heading for a corner of the store where quantities of empty cartons were stacked.

"It's for a giraffe, you see."

Mr. Cowan takes everything in his stride and, quite unruffled, he asked, "How big a giraffe?"

I had never thought when I bought that old-gold giraffe with pink spots at the bazaar what a problem he would present when it came to mailing him to California. His neck was *very* long. Bob was all for winding his neck and head around the rest of him.

"What will that do to his dignity?" I said. What I really meant was his neck wasn't all that firm. He might never again hold up his head.

Mr. Cowan dug out a box that would

308

include neck straight out, or so I guessed, while Bob was selecting a few more boxes for other Christmas presents for the West Coast and the North.

With the boxes stacked in the car we went on out to Lynn—to the yarn shop. Mr. Reid, an ingenious individual, has created an absolutely irresistible store there. He buys up mill ends in all shades and weights. Just to enhance the scene, he arranges great hanks of them outdoors in the sunlight in an assortment of glorious colors. Each day he changes the arrangement. If you love color, and who doesn't, the place draws you like a magnet. I can stand in front of a beautiful combination of three or four shades together and by merely looking at them feel replenished and refreshed. Our idea today was to get some thick yarn in bright tints to tie up Christmas presents. At home afterward with our rolls of yarn, many folds of white tissue, brown paper and heavy string, we happily spread ourselves out on my study floor. I did the inner wrapping; Bob the outer. Preparing a small giraffe, however awkwardly shaped, for a cross-country trip wasn't so bad once we got at it.

How gay the packages look with orange and blue wool and white tissue. I would like to have put in branches of holly with bright red berries but, alas, I've learned that holly doesn't survive a long trip.

A couple of hours later there was our stack of brown-paper wrapped parcels, and Bob started off to the post office.

> God respects me when I work
> God loves me when I sing

writes Radindranath Tagore. I was certainly in the mood for singing this morning when we set out for Charlotte. It's always interesting to visit a town where you've never before been. We had errands —Christmas presents and such. A sparkling brilliant sun shone down as the road led us along beside rolling fields of tawny orange grass, and everywhere a backdrop of blue mountains. In the town of Kings Mountain, bordering the main street, were large, beautiful spreading trees. We were curious because they were shaped like oaks but had the thin narrow leaf of a willow. The foliage was an autumnal golden copper. It's a lovely drive all the way to Charlotte.

What a magnificent store was Ivey's, gay with sparkling Christmas trees, tinsel and twinkling lights. We discovered an appealing shirt for Bob, and nearby a display of umbrellas. Bob's umbrella was falling apart and I'd lost mine so we decided to each give the other one for Christmas. We found one for Bob with a pretty carved wooden handle. You just press something and, magically, it soars aloft. Women's umbrellas came in gay, giddy colors. I passed up the plastic bubble varieties, thinking they might give me claustrophobia, and settled on a bright pumpkin-yellow one that folded up to twelve inches. One I could readily see out from under.

With bundles under our arms we ascended to the restaurant—the Terrace Room—and sat by a window looking down across Charlotte. How slim and lofty were the spires of the old church outside. And sure enough there was another of those marvelous trees, golden copper in the sun. The waitress appeared with the menu and immediately we all became friends. She began by admiring my Zuni Indian necklace and then we were discussing what kind of tree that was outside. She disappeared to get roast beef and baked potatoes and find out about the tree.

The roast beef was rare and delicious and the baked potato heartening after the long drive and busy morning. The tree, we learned, was a willow oak—the same as those we had passed along the main street of Kings Mountain. At mid-afternoon, with an armful of packages, we settled in the car for the long drive home. It had been interesting to wander about a city again, see tall buildings and a degree of traffic. Most of all, it was a joy to be in a sizable city that was free from rush, pressure, and frenzy— a place full of people but still with a feeling of leisure, Southern warmth and gracious friendliness.

All at once, when the last leaf falls, we are keenly aware of the location of our house, on a ridge surrounded by mountains. Through bare trees we now enjoy a superb view of Hogback, Rocky Spur and Melrose. Their outlines as the foliage melts away are soft and furry. From a distance the bare branches that clothe the summits and slopes appear almost feathery. We love seeing these three mountains at all times of day. Each morning the rays of the rising sun leap like flames from peak to peak, touching each one with shades of red—vivid raspberry red. Later in the morning blue shadows play over them. Toward dusk they are violet and stand silhouetted against the sky, sometimes golden and sometimes orange. Nothing is lovelier than these winter sunsets.

With the leaves gone, on the downhill side of our house we look through the woods across the brook and up the next ridge to the friendly lights of neighbors' houses. From our beds at night bare limbs outside the window trace fascinating interweaving patterns against the sky, while stars tangle in the treetops, caught in the branches. On moonlight nights long shadows of slim tall tree trunks everywhere march over the ground.

With the leaves gone, not only do we see the mountains but, as we drive about, we are aware of the many weeping willows. Their yellow foliage clings, swaying slightly in the breeze, and each great tree is a vision of trailing streamers of pure gold.

The paper reports a temperature of

twenty-six here and there, but we haven't had a frost yet and the white camellias bloom on and on. A few strands of the illustrious Thermal Belt must be winding through our garden. When we waken, the rhododendron leaves are sometimes curled but by noon it is fifty-five and the sun beams down, warm and cheerful.

In contrast to the flaming autumn colors, the woodland everywhere now is muted, with its own particular beauty. We have the greens of the pines and, glowing against their soft tones, an occasional single bright red or yellow leaf still attached. In summer, when the leaves are abundant and lush, we forget how many pines there are, but now we see them all. At the tips of the branches brown cones open up to drop seeds. I'm sure there's nothing in nature more wondrous than the curves and whole design of a pine cone. I could study one for long minutes.

Also in winter woods stand the toast-colored oaks. The leaves never completely fall off. Many hold, and hold on till next spring's budding forces them aside. Just like us sometimes. We all tend to hold to an idea or concept or way of doing something, resisting the new until we're pushed into it. Resistant or no, these oaks bring a soft, golden-brown glow to the forest everywhere, a tone that alters in changing lights, is different in sunlight and in shadow, varying from brilliant days to rainy ones when they shine in wetness.

Hiking through the woods these days we feel the resilient earth beneath our feet. Frost doesn't strike deep in the ground here in winter, so the paths are always bouncy to walk on. We can almost sense the goings on two inches down or ten feet under. Above ground nature is quiet and growth is dormant, but walking through our garden I'm remembering the wood hyacinths planted here, the winter aconite there, and those hundred or more crocuses put in some weeks ago, and all the daffodils. Everywhere below the earth's surface intense activity is going on. Roots grow stoutly, in promise of things to come. In fall, October and November, we are filled to overflowing with the richness of the summer just past, the fruits we've enjoyed, the armfuls of flowers we've brought in. And now, in winter, the seasons past are firmly built into our bones and gently live in hearts and memories.

perhaps the woodland evergreens have also absorbed the summer sunlight. Now the laurel, hollies, rhododendron, leucothoe, ivy, seem to give it back to us in the shine and glow the winter sun brings to their foliage.

Out in the garden each morning the feeders are alive with birds, bringing motion and color to an otherwise still area. We trim branches of berry-covered holly to make indoor arrangements. The chrysanthemum we bought a month ago in Spartanburg is still a brilliant gold outside the front door. The air is crisp and cold and when we walk we find ourselves moving along briskly, appreciating mittens and snuggly wool scarves. We like this cold crisp air, we Northerners. I like walking in it. I particularly enjoy the smell of wet leaves along the roadside. The gutters are filled with them and in passing now and again I must pick up a handful and breathe in one of nature's loveliest winter scents. In the early morning when I step out on the terrace to greet the sun I enjoy a few quick deep breaths and feel a tingle of chill in nose and throat.

These days the earth and the terrace brick

are covered with white camellia petals—like touches of snow they lie there, catching the sunlight. The sasanquas are still covered with buds. If frost holds off we shall have them at Christmastime—I wonder, I hope. The chrysanthemums along the fence, which have been lovely for weeks and weeks, are passing by. No frost is killing them but they are tired and bid us adieu. The camellias are our one remaining flower. All month long we've been picking them for ourselves and for neighbors. Never have they been this lovely or this numerous. A silver bowlful, floating, always stands on the dining table. When we go visiting we take some in a small plastic bag. We're apt to come home with the bag filled from our friends' bushes; pink ones we don't have, doubles and singles. Near the camellias is daphne odora, a choice little bush, with buds already tipped with color. I'm sure if I prowled around in the cold leaves I would find daffodil and crocus spears waiting and, in one corner of the garden, the Southern magnolia stands magnificent with glossy green foliage.

As we drive about the small towns in the vicinity—Landrum, Columbus, Saluda,

Rutherfordton—are all putting up their holiday decorations. Giddy tinsel trees and Santa Clauses look down from lamp posts along main streets. Stores are decorating their windows and there's an excitement in the air that always comes before the holidays. I'm happy to get all the shopping and mailing done early and the physical aspects of Christmas behind me. When the outward and "things" end of this season are resolved, we can then relax and give over to what we feel as the great day approaches. Last night we talked to our grandson Jesse and his wife, Camilla, in Massachusetts. They were at the beginning of a blizzard. We invited them to come down and spend Christmas with us. Now we'll wait a few days to see what they can work out. Our daughter is coming and, hopefully, our Marine grandson, Jeff.

The world we inhabit is composed of contrasts and opposites. There is up and down, hot and cold, full and ebb tide, winter and summer and countless more. Life itself is a beautiful mix of opposites, of the practical and the mystical, the physical and the spiritual, the outer and the inner. In us these opposites meet. One of the challenges of living is to see how successfully we can blend them. In our doing and being we ourselves become the blender. December is the season of symbols. And the cross is one of the most significant of all. It has something different to tell each person. I like to think of the cross as a symbol of these opposites. The upright and the horizontal —to me these represent the spiritual and the physical, the intangible and the tangible. On the horizontal we live through our practical activities, dealing with things, places, events and people. But cutting right through these, yet always a part of them, is the upright, the mystical, the spiritual. This is never a part of the physical actually but right in it, deepening it and drawing it into an extra dimension. The upright is the longest member of the cross because it is the most meaningful, symbolizing the reach from down on the earth, and under it, up to Infinity.

While the opposites are meeting in us, we hopefully are unifying and allowing them to merge. Sometimes we're not able to do this. Sometimes there occurs a tearing conflict within us that nearly rips us asunder, when the physical and the spiritual, the tangible and the intangible, fight a battle.

In our days we need a balance between both aspects of living. We cannot thrive and be our true balanced selves if we are too much with either the practical or the mystical. We need the swing back and forth, the merging, the constant awareness of the intangible lodged there in the tangible and vice versa. We need the vital, visible here-and-now quality of the material side of things and the importance of being thoroughly with it. We need both things and feelings and always the awareness that we are the meeting ground of the two.

What a lovely place to live where you waken from an afternoon siesta to find a coconut cake! Such was the way of yesterday. I was in that delicious semi-waking state when I heard the door bell and decided not to answer it. Later I went to step into the car and there on the seat, wonder of wonders, was half a coconut cake wrapped in a plastic bag. I guess my mysterious visitor had remembered the neighbors' dogs and decided not to leave it on the doorstep, but set it in the car. It looks marvelous, and we shall enjoy it for dinner. Maybe I will get a phone call telling me who is responsible. I can't very well go around among my friends asking "Did you leave us a coconut cake?" But I must know!!

Valuable insights come blowing on the wind, sometimes unsought, unheralded, unannounced.

Perhaps I should pause and put this, my newest, into a seventeen-syllable Haiku poem—this thought-provoking bit of wisdom. It would make a fine one. But no, not now. I will tell it instead as it came to me.

I have the most adorable tiny vase maybe three inches high. It looks enchanting with two or three chrysanthemums in it, a single camellia, or a sprig of holly. Being of a lovely round fat shape it holds a lot of water and therefore the flower in it lasts a while. The neck is narrow and seldom can more than a single flower fit in unless the stems are fine and slim. I was emptying it a few minutes ago to wash it out and put away. For over a week on Bob's dresser it had been holding the last large golden chrysanthemum. I was standing by the sink shaking the water out, shaking like mad, little spurts coming with each shake. All of a sudden I stopped shaking, and held the base tipped on its side and the water ran out quietly, easily and twice as fast. I'd been working so hard!

Maybe this is akin to one of my favorite Chinese proverbs.

You do not need a jeweled sword to cut a radish with!

Outside the wind was blowing music through the pines. Trees were bending and swaying as in a dance. I put on my coat and walked a little way along the woodland path, looking up at the blue sky, the trees, and listening. I could hear the brook. From way off somewhere came a bird call and the distant sound of a power saw. I put my hand on the rough bark of an armored pine. I was especially aware of the wind in the branches overhead. Presently I seemed to lose myself and become a part of the forest. I was one with the wind, hearing, sensing, seeing what it was doing, but never seeing it. The wind often suggests to me the qualities of living that are there but that we cannot see. Our mountains in summer are there all around our home. But with leaves on the trees we don't see them. Their strength flows into us, their sturdiness and endurance we catch when needed, we feel their force, even when they are not visible.

Many are the truly important things we cannot see but still believe in. Love, friendship, courage, inner strength, wisdom, intuition—the qualities that are nearer than breathing and a part of each of us though never visible nor tangible. The expression of them through us and our responses are what we experience and sometimes see evidence of in action. It is one of the exciting mysteries of living that when we interrupt our doing and listen and contemplate we can sometimes sense and identify briefly with one of these intangibles. And when we do this we return to our daily activities in a different mood.

Standing among the trees, with the wind on my face, I was experiencing one of those transcending moments we're all open to when our minds and spirits are loosed from their usual route. It is occasionally then that our being and our depths emerge to blend with our outer surroundings.

Christmas draws nearer. Each year I know

our tree was never lovelier. This season it is a soft furry long-needle pine that Bob got at the 4-H Club Christmas tree sale. He set the trunk down in the center hole of the terrace millstone table. The tree covers the millstone and is about four feet high. It's strung with tiny white lights which when turned on slowly wink. We must get a star for the topmost branch.

We drove up into the mountains yesterday to cut pine boughs. Later, while Bob was setting up the tree and wiring it firm, I made a little Christmas tree for the front door. Some years ago at a garden club workshop I learned how to make these. You get a piece of plywood and cut it into a triangle the shape of a tree with two long sides reaching up to a peak. Bob had spread and attached chicken wire across the face of it. Beginning at the bottom you slide twigs of pine branch under the wire, overlapping the pieces, until you get to the top and then you have a little two-dimensional pine tree that fits flat against the door itself. A touch of tinsel and a large red bow at the bottom complete the decoration.

We haven't bought any mistletoe yet because the mountain people usually come around with it just before Christmas. It grows high in the oaks and other trees and is visible now everywhere in the area. I don't know how they ever reach it. I've heard they shoot mistletoe down. This I'd love to watch. In any case we're eagerly awaiting the men who bring it, and hope they remember us.

It's ten days before Christmas. Last night we decided to make more banana bread. Bob said he'd mash the bananas while I mingled the other ingredients. This provided a beautiful evening of fragrance in our house and, before we went to bed, six more loaves on the kitchen counter. I was pondering on how happy I was to finish up the mechanical and practical aspects of Christmas well ahead of time so we could merge with the mystical and spiritual side of this significant occasion. But then I began to think—how can you separate the two? You can't. All the while we were mingling up the ingredients for our bread I was thinking of the people we were going to take it to. When you shop and wrap gifts the recipient is clearly in mind as your love flows to him or her or them. If Christmas could be said to be about any one thing it would be about love. And this is what you feel in all the preparations.

Jesse and Camilla just phoned. Not only is Joan coming down, but this beloved young couple too. We also had a phone call from our Marine grandson, Jeffrey. The young never write—they phone. But now that they are adults it is no longer collect! Progress! We are going to have a beautiful family time. Thinking ahead to their arrival gives us a feeling of pure contentment.

Last night it rained three inches and was still pouring this morning. This is a day to make, not one already made. Sometimes you wake and the day is there, beautiful weatherwise, already made, irresistible. You must go out right away and certain things invite doing. But this day was a challenge: dim, rainy and cold. Sometimes these days turn out to be the best of all. These days we make ourselves by ourselves. It is a challenge to see how creative we can be.

What ideal weather for receiving presents, I thought. And what a good time to take people gifts. Bob had a slightly dim view of this idea, having planned to settle at his desk. But I coaxed. Our newly baked six loaves of banana bread were there. Why not deliver them this morning and pay short visits in the process? We had other packages too. We could take them all. And what a good day to go to Ayers's nursery for poinsettias.

Bundled in raincoats and rubbers we set forth. We were just about the only people abroad. The roads were running in rivers and the gutters sloshing along with slightly red water. How green everything looked in the rain. The windshield wiper was busily humming as we sped down toward Ayers. We were cordially welcomed by Mrs. Ayers and complimented on our courage in coming out in such weather. We were, of course, the only customers in the shop. After we'd talked a few moments we moved to the greenhouse. There before us was a solid bank of red poinsettias. The entire greenhouse was filled with them, each one touching the next and every plant covered with blooms. They seemed to bring their own brilliance and sunlight to the spot. We stood in wonder before such color and beauty and all the while the rain with a kind of stippeling sound came down on the glass roof. There were red poinsettias, a marvelous Chinese red; pink ones, a soft smoky pink that were absolutely irresistible; and white ones. We walked up and down the aisles, absorbing the vibrancy and vitality on all sides, and selecting which to buy. I yearned for a pink for the living room but not with the old-gold rug, I feared. However, we had a friend just back from the hospital who has a pink-and-blue living room so we chose one for her and a red one for ourselves, and a pot of glorious bronzy-yellow chrysanthemums from a far corner for another couple.

What a lovely morning we had. When we got home, the poinsettia brought the whole living room to life in a very special way. The blossoms look even bigger here than in the nursery. By actual measure, they are sixteen inches across.

There's a beautiful atmosphere of Christmas everywhere. We think Tryon has the prettiest decorations of all. Along the main street at intervals stand large full Christmas trees, each covered with multi-colored lights.

Around the bank dogwoods are lit with tiny white lights and a large Christmas tree similarly lit stands nearby. The stage is beautifully set and the air of Christmas is not only in decorations but all through the town. You are aware of a great warmth in the stores. There is hustle and bustle and tinsel and tissue but under all this we meet a friendliness and gaiety that is contagious. Perhaps because Tryon is a small town there is lacking the sense of pressure and fatigue that one usually finds in large city stores before Christmas. In contrast, here the stores are meeting places for all ones friends. Each shopping expedition is a social occasion at any season, but especially now, and because it's Christmas many people are abroad.

We were walking on the mountain road just above our house one brisk and chilly afternoon recently when a car stopped. A truck, with three smiling black men in the front seat. In the back were great cartons of mistletoe and holly. They hadn't forgotten us!

"Merry Christmas, you all," they called.

"Wouldn't you like some mistletoe?" the driver asked. One of the other men had jumped out and began handing us great green branches, each one glowing wlth shiny translucent white berries.

"Merry Christmas to *you*, and we certainly would," I replied, admiring each bunch, till we had an armful.

"Which is the prettiest?" We were comparing this one with that.

"How did you ever get up the tree to get these, or did you shoot them down?" I asked. I wanted to prolong this pleasant encounter.

"No shooting. We climbed. You should have seen us."

"We were like a batch of monkeys," the third member chimed in.

Bob and I selected two beautiful bunches, large and very full, for which we paid a dollar. Then the leader said, "So there, give them another for a Christmas present." They handed us another cluster, enormous, the size of all that we had together. I am remembering the small, wizened twigs available in the supermarkets in northern city areas—a bare handful in plastic for several dollars.

We took a bunch on up the hill to Meggie and Jack. They are old friends and their children used to play with our children thirty years or so ago down here. They were delighted with the holiday greenery and we sat and talked a while.

On the way home we met another friend driving up the mountain to her home. Her husband is in the hospital, having had a serious heart attack. We asked her how things were going.

"Touch and go, until today," she said. "Now he *really* looks better—he has turned the corner, thank God."

Ann looked exhausted, but also relieved. What courage people display when they meet a challenge like this. She had had a rough week which she had met with her usual stamina and we were happy to hear of the improvement.

As we neared our house with arms full of mistletoe, we heard a loud explosion, and a jeep minus a muffler roared past. Oh yes, the neighbors' teenagers are back from college. And now we are home, and just across the street from us John's tree is lighted up. It's the pine along his drive with tiny colored lights all over it, each one shaped like a rose, and the whole effect pure enchantment.

Turning in toward our front door we see Charles coming down the street—another neighbor, and a very fine artist. We wait to congratulate him on the award he has just received for one of his pictures on exhibition in Paris.

These are our people, I thought. These are our mountains. This is our home: and here our roots reach down, deeper and deeper all the time.

Today Bob made a fish chowder—a great bowlful to freeze and have when the family comes. I made orange jello with real oranges and then an apple pie. After supper we walked across the street to John's. Homer was there and we sat and talked by the fire a while. They confessed that they had brought over the coconut cake. What could two bachelors do with a present of a huge coconut cake? So they had halved it.

One end of the kitchen is all plastic pails and boxes filled with fresh new terrarium material. The temperature is twenty degrees outside and so we have to keep it all indoors. We have had our first frost now and the camellias are dead and brown. But the sun is shining brilliantly and the mountains are clear and sharp against a blue, blue sky.

Yesterday Betty and I went for terrarium

material. We had awakened to pouring rain. But Betty is one of those undaunted people, and I rather like rain myself, so we set forth in their Volkswagen bus with pails, trowels, plastic bags, and so on in back.

Betty looked like something straight from the moon! She had on rubber boots, a great poncho covering her head and reaching to her feet, and a jaunty red plastic fireman's hat. I wasn't nearly as colorful with my winter coat and raincoat and rain hat, but well protected. We drove down the Pacolet valley to a place Betty knew where an acre of partridgeberry grew along a river bank. The nearer we got to our goal the wetter it looked. As we arrived the heavens let go and we could scarcely see a few feet in front of us. So we sat by the road waiting for it to stop and had a beautiful conversation. Of course, it never did let up and after a while we decided to go home and begin over another day when the weather cleared.

Next day was sunny and beautiful, but cool, just thirty-two. We were prepared with woolies, sweaters and mittens. The mountains were clear enough to reach out and touch. The hillside of partridgeberry was covered with wet leaves that we must burrow into thereby soaking and freezing our fingers.   No berries anywhere.

"Impossible!" exclaimed Betty.   "There are always berries here." But we gave up and retreated to the car to thaw out. While a welcome sun shone in on us we talked about our childhoods; Betty's here in Tryon and mine in New York along the Hudson. I was fascinated to learn about Christmas here a number of years ago.

We hadn't really given up and when we got warm we set forth again. This time we discovered berries. Here and there they crept through the leaves. First we would see a single red one. parting the leaves at that spot, we discover several more. We listened to the sound of the river flowing below us and felt the sun's warmth. On this southern slope we were out of the wind. Roaming over the hillside we filled plastic bags, taking an inch or so of stem with each berry. If we pulled no roots we would not harm these plants on the protected list. Lovely stumps we discovered too, and in some places the partridgeberry grew up clothing part of the stump with green vine, brightened here and there with a scarlet berry.

When we had all we needed we continued

farther along the Pacolet River and came across banks of mosses and lichen, tiny ferns, all sorts of treasures. Here a piece of bark with lichen on it, there British soldiers, red tipped, and the green fairy cups lichen, moss short haired and smooth, moss long haired and furry to touch.

About noon, our baskets filled with greenery, we headed home. I watered the trays and bags of material and set them all in one end of the kitchen. Too cold to leave them outside. Now I am all ready to make terrariums.

Christmastime is magic and marvels and wonders. We are at a dinner party, long dresses and candlelight, pine boughs and silver stars and shining silver on the snowy tablecloth. The smell of an open fire, white curtains drawn close, laughter, the warmth of close friends. And outside, on the way home, a full moon shining down, and stars, and black mountains silhouetted against the sky. The fragrance of other peoples' pinewood fires drifts to us as we drive past houses where we see the warm, golden glow of houselights through partly closed curtains.

On Trade Street each day people are carrying packages. Families gather from far and near. Young people continually stream home from colleges. Stars light up the eyes of small children. Each mail brings parcels and we put them on the cupboard in my study. They come from our children in California and from old friends in the North. We take off the outside wrappings to reveal red and green tissue, bright labels. Some packages are lumpy and heavy, some are light. Mystery and curiosity abound. This is the month the stars seem brightest of the whole year as they shine down over the mountains. A friend brings us a delicate feathery silver star, skillfully cut from a tin can—just what we wanted. Bob attaches it to the top of the outside tree.

Some days later, with a temperature of sixty, I settled on the terrace to make terrariums. A terrarium is a lovely object for the house in winter and a much appreciated present to friends at Christmas.

From the cellar of the Blue Ridge Weavers gift shop last week they had brought up brandy breathers in clear glass, dusty and unused. I had washed them in ammonia and detergent and polished them till they shone. All the treasures Betty and I had found in the Pacolet valley were spread around me on the terrace benches. Bits of gray reindeer moss, clusters of partridgeberry, tiny ebony spleenwort fern, pipsissewa, rattlesnake plantains, bits of lichen. With my precious long-handled tweezers I arranged and re-arranged, creating in each glass bowl a miniature woodland scene.

There I was, surrounded by the mountains which formed a macrocosm, and dealing with a little row of microcosms, tiny worlds within glass. Now, for a moment, I myself am miniscule, less than an inch high, and I walk through my terrariums, along this path here, climbing up over that smooth green mound, through a tangle of blue moss, pausing to rest on a half-inch hemlock cone, wading through long-haired moss, walking on smooth, short-haired green moss. I am in a small dell with a great fern towering over me and the pattern of a rattlesnake plantain leaf large beside me.

In the grayness of the midwinter dawn I am up in a silent house. Bob is still asleep. The rim of sky beyond the mountains is a deep orange streak tangling through the gray. I hear the trills of a cardinal in a treetop somewhere. They perch high to sing, and here they sing off and on all winter.

The dim shapes of the trees outside loom up: packages wrapped for Christmas glisten in the lamplight. The house waits. I wait. A few more days now and Joan will be here—and Jeff, our Marine, and Jesse and Camilla. These are the grandchildren who used to snuggle close and warm and listen with large eyes to bedtime stories. Now they are grown. We shall be a family of six and these delicious days just beforehand are filled with anticipation, with all their mystery and magic, with all their wonder and silent joy. In the very air is a beautiful sense of waiting, of being ready to give and share, and at the same time of being open and ready to receive. Christmas is an abundance of both giving and receiving. I often think Christmas is rather like a cross between a great wave that comes over us all and a marvelous kind of brain shampoo, the sort that leaves your mind and spirits fresh, clean-scrubbed, sun-dried.

The wave is something we go under if we are in love with this season and we are.

When we emerge something new is with us; this great annual far-flung happening is always one of the year's peaks.

So it was this season.

I am remembering those delicious ripples that began a few days before the day of first arrivals as Bob and I gathered our forces, thought of food, last-minute shopped, and planned. The initial stirrings begun early in the month continued to grow and build. There were letters and phone calls about arrivals and plans and lengths of stay. Jesse and Camilla will stay at Oak Hall. Jeff also. Joan will be with us. We will eat some meals at the hotel and they will eat some with us. We have food in the freezer and in the refrigerator and of course Christmas dinner will be at our house. Distant presents were long since mailed and local ones delivered; visiting family presents wrapped. Now, with the practical aspects of the holiday successfully coped with, we felt the great wave come to engulf us, and we welcomed it.

The arrival of Jesse and Camilla two days ahead of the others was the beginning. What happens to me when beloved family comes is I simply move out of my orbit into theirs.

This is a very interesting experience, and as refreshing and stimulating as a trip to another country. Maybe that's what it is. Certainly from our realm of retirement to the age of college is a different country and a long journey.

All at once after Jesse and Camilla arrived I became a senior at Amherst, then a new wife. All their plans, interests and activities absorb and swallow us up, and we love it. We haven't seen them since their wedding a year ago. We move through their apartment with them as they describe it, and draw a floor plan. I am attending classes with Jesse at college. We go with them to their study group center in Vermont where they spend nearly every weekend. We stand poised on the brink of graduation with Jesse, aware of an alertness and a what next? feeling—what job, what kind of work or career—who knows? They are generous in sharing their lives, interests, excitements and challenges.

Together we write Haiku, the familiar seventeen-syllable Japanese poetry. What lovely images their poetry evokes. We turn on Mahler's Symphony no. 4 and the four of us experience together Creative Motion in dim lights. We move freely about the room as the music suggests. We give each other neck and back rubs on the rug in front of the fire before going to bed. One evening we reveled in a luscious candlelight roast beef dinner at Oak Hall. An enchanted two days in a different world.

Camilla had never been South before. With her we felt again those same first reactions, the joy of the warmth and friendliness of Oak Hall and the unique hospitality of Clara Edwards, who runs it. The spirit of the South, the leisure and slower tempo, reached out to touch Camilla even at the airport, and as she talked of it we remembered our first visits here and our similar reactions.

Two of our favorite friends come for the evening and we six share ideas on every level. Jesse and Camilla are wonderful in explaining the especially meaningful aspects of their current studies. We try to reach through a new (to us) group of terms to understand the spirit that guides them. We all agree that there is but one mountain we are all climbing, but many, many paths up it, and that we are each drawn to the path that is right for us. What a privilege to have, through these intelligent, keenly alert young people, one foot in the current scene—their current scene.

We took them on our favorite walks, explored the twin lakes trail, and the path to Melrose Falls. And we took them food-shopping to give them the feel of the town itself.

Another element was added when Jeff, age twenty-one, arrived from his Marine base, wrapped in an aura of the military. Again we touched a new scene, a new way of life. We hadn't seen him in a year, either. We heard all about his six-months' cruise to the Mediterranean, details of his adventures exploring Florence, Pisa and Venice on leave and his responses to Greece and Spain. With him we faced his future when he leaves the Marines in July. We listened to his plans.

After we had absorbed his very special and individual personality into our midst, Joan joined us. She comes in a glorious burst of enthusiasm, bringing tales of her deep interest in English country dancing and recorder playing, both of which she teaches at a school on Long Island.

We sing carols, play the recorder by the fire in the candlelight, walk mountain trails together. We haven't seen Joan for seven months and are spellbound listening to the adventures of her group dancing on the New York Public Library steps this fall, and in Central Park on Sundays last summer. There they invited anyone and everyone to participate and taught all passersby who wanted to join in.

Christmas is the time of listening. We have listened to each of these family members, to their stories to be sure, but to much more. When you really listen you hear more than words. You hear beyond words, beyond outward activities to what each one is, who he is, where he is now, where he is reaching, where he is headed. New depths in family relationships are touched and explored. All the while we have totally left our private twosome world and merged with life at its beginnings with the young people and at midpoint with Joan.

Yes, this is a time of taking in and receiving. But while we listen and step into this younger world, we never completely lose ourselves. We find ourselves stretching the horizons of our own lives, remodeling our acceptances to take in some of the current ways that are entirely different from those we followed when we were twenty-one and twenty-two or in our mid-forties.

Christmas dinner, and we had it a day ahead, was roast beef and creamed onions, peas, enormous olives, mince pie, candlelight and carols. To dignify the occasion, we all dressed up, we women in long dresses. Then we went as a family to the Christmas Eve midnight service. The church was full—candlelight, the fragrance of pine boughs, and rich clusters of red poinsettias at the altar. I could feel my spirits rise and soar with the upreaching lines of nave and chancel. I felt one with everyone there, with family and with the Power greater than us all that permeated the service and all those in the church, lifting us beyond ourselves, and into being more than we are. And now the organ played my favorite carol, Oh, Little Town of Bethlehem. Sung by the full choir, and the full congregation, the music and voices inspired and held us high.

We had our Christmas a day ahead because on Christmas day itself a general dispersal of family occurred with plans and schedules uppermost in the minds of all.

An interesting couple arrived to drive Joan over to a week-long dance festival at

Berea in Kentucky. They had driven from Vermont in two days. This was startling enough but even more so was the fact that they lived up there in a tree-house with no plumbing, no heat, no electricity, and the year round.

"When the snow is up to my waist, it is tiring to push through," the attractive, enthusiastic young woman told us. "But it isn't usually that deep. I can make it easily when it's only knee high."

We stepped into yet another world in their short stay and felt a part of these two lives.

Christmas night Betty and Norme had a party for all ages and we sat around their lighted tree and fire sharing our peak moments of the year just past. After a little while Betty asked, "If you had a present of six months, unlimited health, wealth, abilities, and no obstacles, what would you do?"

"Walk the Appalachian Trail," said thirteen-year-old Curtis, with no hesitation.

"Travel all over Europe with a guitar and a teacher who could teach me how to play as I went," said a young mother of teenagers.

"Visit Nepal and Tibet and live on a houseboat in Kashmir," was mine. (I once saw at Asia House in New York an unforgettable Buddha from Nepal.)

"Go around the world on a yacht stopping for a while wherever there are horses," from a pretty, pretty teenager.

"Travel the Northwest in our camper," said Norme, our host.

We all agreed that we wanted to spend our own chosen six months but everyone else's also.

We thought we might as well include New Year's too in this gala evening so we all wrote on a blank card a New Year's resolution for someone else in the room and anonymous, no name of who it was for or from. These were read aloud and we tried to guess who each one was written for. It was most amusing, and sometimes several of us claimed the same resolution. All the while the fire glowed, the Christmas tree lights twinkled and outside stars shone down.

"Pray God bless all friends here. A merry, merry Christmas and a happy New Year," everyone sang as we went out the door to drive home under the stars.

Now Bob and I are alone. All the new presents are incorporated into our lives and no longer piled here and there; new books have been started and most things are back in place. The cuckoo clock ticks, the utilities hum, a fire glows on the hearth, while outdoors holly leaves shine in the moonlight, and a few last buds on the sasanqua camellias unfold snowy white.

Today I am in bed relaxing, enjoying our aloneness and solitude, reliving all the delicious scenes of recent happenings.

We are gradually emerging from the wave. I see now the same shore line as before they all came but, someway, it is different too, perhaps because we are a little different. We have taken in so much that is fresh and new. How could anything ever be quite the same, or anyone?

We have given and received. We have listened and heard. Something fresh and new has been added. We have been under our Christmas wave, and now our minds and spirits feel fresh, clean-scrubbed, snowy white, and sun-dried.

THE END

Large Print Inspirational Books from Walker

Would you like to be on our Large Print mailing list? Please send your name and address to:

B. Walker
Walker and Company
720 Fifth Avenue
New York, NY 10019

A Book of Hours

Elizabeth Yates

The Alphabet of Grace

Frederick Buechner

The Adventure of Spiritual Healing

Michael Drury

A Certain Life: Contemporary Meditations on the Way of Christ

Herbert O'Driscoll

A Gathering of Hope

Helen Hayes

Getting Through the Night: Finding Your Way After the Loss of a Loved One

Eugenia Price

Inner Healing: God's Great Assurance

Theodore Dobson

Instrument of Thy Peace

Alan Paton

The Irrational Season

Madeleine L'Engle

Jonathan Livingston Seagull

Richard Bach

Living Simply Through the Day

Tilden Edwards

The Power of Positive Thinking

Norman Vincent Peale

The Touch of the Earth

Jean Hersey

Gift From the Sea

Anne Morrow Lindbergh

A Grief Observed

C.S. Lewis

A Guide to Christian Meditation

Marilyn Morgan Helleberg

Up From Grief

Bernardine Kreis and Alice Pattie

Walking With Loneliness

Paula Ripple

The Way of the Wolf

Martin Bell

Who Will Deliver Us?

Paul Zahl

With Open Hands

Henri Nouwen

Words of Certitude

Pope John Paul II

Words to Love By

Mother Teresa

The Sacred Journey

Frederick Buechner

Something Beautiful for God

Malcolm Muggeridge

Strength to Love

Martin Luther King, Jr.

To God Be the Glory

Billy Graham and
Corrie Ten Boom